AMONGST THE ALPHAS

by LINKED IN AND TOWN HALL ACHIEVER OF THE YEAR
EY NOMINEE ENTREPRENEUR OF THE YEAR
GRAND HOMAGE LYS DIVERSITY
WORLD TOP100 DOCTORS

Dr BAK NGUYEN, DMD

&

Dr. MARIA KUNSTADTER, DMD
Dr. PAUL OUELLETTE, DDS, MS, ABO, AFAAID
Dr. JEREMY KRELL, DMD, MBA

TO ALL THOSE LOOKING TO WALK THEIR DESTINY AND WANDERING WHY THEY ARE SO DIFFERENT.

by Dr BAK NGUYEN

Copyright © 2021 Dr BAK NGUYEN

All rights reserved.

ISBN: 978-1-989536-33-9

Published by: Dr. BAK PUBLISHING COMPANY
Dr.BAK 0058

DISCLAIMER

« The general information, opinions and advice contained in this medium and/or the books, audiobooks, podcasts and publications on Dr. Bak Nguyen's (legal name Dr. Ba Khoa Nguyen) website or social media (hereinafter the "Opinions") present general information on various topics. The Opinions are intended for informational purposes only.

No information contained in the Opinions is a substitute for an expert, consultation, advice, diagnosis or professional treatment. No information contained in the Opinions is a substitute for professional advice and should not be construed as consultation or advice.

Nothing in the Opinions should be construed as professional advice related to the practice of dentistry, medical advice or any other form of advice, including legal or financial advice, professional opinion, care or diagnosis, but strictly as general information. All information from the Opinions is for informational purposes only.

Any user who disagrees with the terms of this Disclaimer should immediately cease using or referring to the Opinions. Any action by the user in connection with the information contained in the Opinions is solely at the user's discretion.

The general information contained in the Opinions is provided "as is" and without warranty of any kind, either expressed or implied. Dr. Bak Nguyen (legal name Dr. Ba Khoa Nguyen) makes every effort to ensure that the information is complete and accurate. However, there is no guarantee that the general information contained in the Opinions is always available, truthful, complete, up-to-date or relevant.

The Opinions expressed by Dr. Bak Nguyen (legal name Dr. Ba Khoa Nguyen) are personal and expressed in his own name and do not reflect the opinions of his companies, partners and other affiliates.

Dr. Bak Nguyen (legal name Dr. Ba Khoa Nguyen) also disclaims any responsibility for the content of any hyperlinks included in the Opinions.

Always seek the advice of your expert advisors, physicians or other qualified professionals with any questions you may have regarding your condition. Never disregard professional advice or delay in seeking it because of something you have read, seen or heard in the Opinions. »

ABOUT THE AUTHORS

From Canada, **Dr. BAK NGUYEN**, Nominee Ernst and Young Entrepreneur of the year, Grand Homage Lys DIVERSITY, LinkedIn & TownHall Achiever of the year and TOP 100 Doctors 2021. Dr Bak is a cosmetic dentist, CEO and founder of Mdex & Co. His company is revolutionizing the dental field. Speaker and motivator, he wrote 72 books over 36 months accumulating many world records (to be officialized). His books are covering:

- **ENTREPRENEURSHIP**
- **LEADERSHIP**
- **QUEST OF IDENTITY**
- **DENTISTRY AND MEDICINE**
- **PARENTING**
- **CHILDREN'S BOOKS**
- **PHILOSOPHY**

In 2003, he founded Mdex, a dental company upon which in 2018, he launched the most ambitious private endeavour to reform the dental industry, Canada wide. Philosopher, he has close to his heart the quest of happiness of the people surrounding him, patients and colleagues alike. In 2020, he launched an International collaborative initiative named **THE ALPHAS** to share knowledge and for Entrepreneurs and Doctors to thrive through the Greatest Pandemic and Economic depression of our time.

In 2016, he co-found with Tranie Vo, Emotive World Incorporated, a tech research company to use technology to empower happiness and sharing. U.A.X. the ultimate audio experience is the landmark project on which the team is advancing, utilizing the technics of the movie industry and the advancement in ARTIFICIAL INTELLIGENCE to save the book industry and to upgrade the continuing education space.

These projects have allowed Dr Nguyen to attract interests from the international and diplomatic community and he is now the center of a global discussion in the wellbeing and the future of the health profession. It is in that matter that he shares his thoughts and encourages the health community to share their own stories.

"It's not worth it go through it alone! Together, we stand, alone, we fall."

Motivational speaker and serial entrepreneur, philosopher and author, from his own words, Dr Nguyen describes himself as a dentist by circumstances, an entrepreneur by nature and a communicator by passion.

He also holds recognitions from the Canadian Parliament and the Canadian Senate.

ABOUT THE GUEST AUTHORS

From USA, **Dr. Maria Kunstadter**, Doctor of Dental Surgery, co-founder THE TELEDENTIST, the biggest TELEDENTISTRY provider in USA. Experienced President with a demonstrated history of working in the hospital & health care industry. Skilled in Customer Service, Sales, Strategic Planning, Team Building, and Public Speaking. Strong business development professional with a Doctor of Dental Surgery focused in Advanced General Dentistry from UMKC School of Dentistry.

From USA: **Dr. Paul Ouellette**, DDS, MS, ABO, AFAAID, WORLD TOP 100 DENTISTS, Former Associate Professor Georgia School of Orthodontics and Jacksonville University. A visionary man looking for the future of our profession. Dr. Paul Ouellette Highly motivated to help my sons become successful in the "Ouellette Family of Dentists" Group Dental Specialty Practice.

From USA, **Dr. Jeremy Krell**, dentist MBA and serial entrepreneur, the real definition of an OVERACHIEVER. Highly experienced innovator and entrepreneur with a proven track record of taking early-stage startups to acquisition (multi-million dollar buyout). Excellent clinical dentistry and communication skills with in-depth analytical, organizational, and problem-solving abilities. A detail orientated and strategic leader in a dynamic, expeditious innovative environment. Firm experience with strategy, positioning companies, leading & developing teams, raising capital, investor relations, dental materials & techniques, negotiating & closing deals, and sales.

by Dr. BAK NGUYEN
with Dr. MARIA KUNSTADTER,
Dr. PAUL OUELLETTE
& Dr. JEREMY KRELL

INTRODUCTION
BY Dr BAK NGUYEN

WHAT IS AN ALPHA?
CHAPTER 1 - Dr. BAK NGUYEN

HOW DO ALPHAS RECOGNIZE EACH OTHER?
CHAPTER 2 - Dr. BAK NGUYEN

HOW DO YOU DEAL WITH ALPHAS?
CHAPTER 3 - Dr. BAK NGUYEN

ARE ALPHAS PROTECTORS?
CHAPTER 4 - Dr. BAK NGUYEN

WHAT DO ALPHAS SACRIFICE?
CHAPTER 5 - Dr. BAK NGUYEN

THE ALPHA GENE?
CHAPTER 6 - Dr. BAK NGUYEN

THE EVOLUTION OF THE ALPHA?
CHAPTER 7 - Dr. BAK NGUYEN

ARE THERE MANY TYPES OF ALPHAS?
CHAPTER 8 - Dr. BAK NGUYEN

PART II
BY GUEST AUTHORS

ALPHAS I KNOW AND LOVE?
CHAPTER 9 - Dr. MARIA KUNSTADTER

PROUD TO BE AN ALPHA
CHAPTER 10 - Dr. PAUL OUELLETTE

OPPORTUNITY: BY ALPHAS, FOR ALPHAS
CHAPTER 11 - Dr. JEREMY KRELL

CONCLUSION
BY Dr BAK NGUYEN

INTRODUCTION
by Dr. BAK NGUYEN

What a great feeling to be back! After a month trying to beat my last world records (4 within a month), and trying to repeat history to celebrate a world record with more world records (in 2018, I celebrated a **15 books written within 15 months** world record, writing **8 children's books** in a month with William), I am both exhausted and disappointed.

We do have 22k words written for the **BOOK OF LEGENDS VOL. 3**, while the general public is discovering the first volume. Within a month, we have set up the worlds, the sets, the characters, even the soundtracks of the **WORLD OF ETO**, our new franchise, but neither the **BOOK OF LEGENDS** is completed, neither any Teen's book yet.

It is not the **WILL** that was missing, it was the stamina and… the Momentum. William and I drafted 2 stories, but there are still to be written into words, actions, and emotions.

For the last few weeks, I felt… incompetent, useless. It is not fair, will you tell me. I tried that too! Everyone is entitled to some rest, especially after such a run (56 books written within 27 months!) I slept more, I even have time to watch TV. I should have felt rest, but I hated the feeling.

> "To feel heavy and useless is the worst punishment to a driver, an Alpha."
> Dr. Bak Nguyen

For my defence, it was the Christmas holidays. Even then, I managed to secure the composition of my Board of Directors with 3 of the greatest minds in the country in Technology, Medicine, and Finance.

I entertained my kid, teaching him the art and the craft of scriptwriting. But it wasn't until I finally walked back into my boardroom, the **BOARD OF INFLUENCE**, that I found myself whole again, for the first time in weeks.

Yesterday was my first executive meeting with my officers. The first board that will launch the year, the first meeting that will set the pace. Actually, I had 4 meetings back to back that day. It felt good! I was back at my true self…

Amongst my trusted officers, coach Jonas Diop was at the table. We reconnected just where we left, a few weeks ago, right before the holidays. The last time that we met, he was signing copies of **MASTERMIND**, my 52nd book, and our first one together!

Are you ready to do it again? I never heard his answer, we were already planning the title and the dateline. **AMONGST THE ALPHAS** will be our next chapter together.

At first, I wasn't sure about the subject, **ALPHAS**? Jonas, on the other hand, was determined to have me answering his questions. There is no doubt in his mind that I have to share my experience, feelings, and thoughts on the matter.

To him, this is not only about sharing, but about understanding the pressure, the pleasure, the pain, and the distinction of being an Alpha.

I must say that I was flattered, but by now, I just need an opportunity to jump back at my Momentum! By the next morning, around 8 AM, I received by SMS, a list of 15 questions on the matter of being an Alpha.

From my yesterday's meetings, I had at least 5 books on the table plus all of the derivative work coming with them (videos, podcasts, seminars, etc). On top of it, I still haven't finished my books with William yet.

At 8 AM, I received the questions. On my way to work, I got a phone call from a fan I connected with on LinkedIn, a few months earlier. She invited me to speak to entrepreneurs and company owners on how to incorporate diversity harmoniously into their workforce. That was an invite from an affiliate of the immigration department. That was yesterday on the way to work.

This morning, before I could go through Jonas' list of questions, I received another invite, this time, to speak in front of a crowd of 600 teenagers, to share with them how I succeeded, and to inspire them to do the same.

I could have asked why me? But why the self compliment? Instead, I responded kindly, how can I help? I guess this is what it means to be an Alpha. We are different, we inspire, we can have people talking about us, against us, for us; it doesn't matter, we do not leave anyone indifferent.

By the time I sat down in my office taking my coffee, I had the cover finished. **AMONGST THE ALPHAS**, this is my 58th book. It is time to come back to my nature, to my core. And what about the other books, William's books?

Rest assured, I never give up. Let's just say that I will take a little pause for a few days to start and finish this one first.

> "To keep Momentum, aim for your next win as soon as possible."
> Dr. Bak Nguyen

In other words, let go for what's easy first. To write about leadership, philosophy, mindset, and business, that's natural, that's easy. Let's find our footing from there first, and rising the Momentum up, so as the winds are favorable, our sails (William and I) will be ready to relaunch in a near future.

Without further due, what is an Alpha? While I was looking for an image for the cover, I stumbled upon a famous painting of the French revolution: a half-naked woman holding the flag of freedom with a young kid holding a musket by her side. I hesitated for a long moment. This is not representative of an Alpha!

Surprised? This is how we like to see and to paint our leaders, as courageous risk takers that will fight against and despite all the odds. Well, as true as it is part of the nature of an Alpha, it is merely a fraction of who and what we are.

We aren't fighters, even if we do not shy away from a fight. We are builders, we are dreamers, we are the eternal hopes that the best is yet to come. We fight only to go through. We have opponents, but we have the ability not to make it personal.

Are we strong? Not by nature. We became strong out of necessity to keep the flame alive and burning. Are we looking to defy? Not at all. We are looking to help, to improve, to build. The fight comes as we meet with the **wall of Pride** and the **shadow of FEAR and IGNORANCE**.

"It is not wisdom but Authority that makes a law."
Thomas Hobbes

That's how we will come to fight. Not because we are fighters nor because we need to win at all cost, but because we are believers and we won't back down in front of adversity, intimidation, or laziness.

If that's what you call courage, well, most of us had to learn courage on the way. We weren't born courageous, we became courageous out of necessity.

Are we revolutionaries looking to burn down the house? Absolutely not. On the contrary, our main nature is to help. If it is easy, that it seems effortless to achieve, it is often because it wasn't about us! We did it to serve and to help the others, that's how growing was less painful.

Yes, we do it because it is our nature, it is who we are and how we breathe. We do it to evolve, we do it to help and to serve. On the way, I grew bigger and stronger, almost painlessly, or so it seems.

This is a great introduction to the Alphas. Even if we received it as a core at birth, we all chose to embrace our nature or not.

> "One cannot train into an Alpha. One can only accept who he or she truly is, and let it flourish."
> Dr. Bak Nguyen

So being an Alpha is not a status, it is a choice, once we came to terms with our true nature. For decades, I let my parents and my surroundings convinced me that I was a disruptive force, not able to fit in line. I sincerely do not know how I became a doctor.

Love, much love, was needed from both sides. They never gave up on me, giving me all of their affection and hopes, trying to ... heal me. I love them, I tried my best to fit in, erasing my pain with company and society.

40 years later, it all came crumbling down. The only thing that stood tall was the warm feeling of love and the souvenir of the good intentions.

Most of my training was holding me down. Most of my beliefs were false, partial and yet, inflexible. Most of my code source were corrupted and incomplete. I rose into an Alpha the day I forgave myself and embraced who I really was.

You all know how I remedy to the failing system. I rebooted it, embracing the **YESMAN CHALLENGE** for 18 months. I threw away most of my sorting system and all the filters too. I raised questions about everything, even on the smallest of matters, and was ready for new answers.

"One must learn to build before he should destroy." That's common wisdom, that sounds great, but how do you apply it in everyday life?

Well, in my quest to reboot myself, I not only threw away the subjects but also most of the instructions on how to gather information and how to evaluate it.

It is not enough to want to change. It is not enough to do things differently. If one wants to grow and to change genuinely, one must be ready to be flexible about how he evaluates his own results.

This should be a quote, but since it is so long, I wasn't sure how to formulate it. It just went out as is. I guess I will let you the honor to polish it.

This is how I made peace with myself, how I finally freed myself from the **chains of conformity**, love, and peer pressure. Peacefully and with determination, I rose up, let go of my chains and false beliefs, and embraced without hate nor regrets my true nature, one you call an Alpha.

I won't be making Alphas out of you. On the other hand, I will help you understand the feeling and the consequences. If you are still reading (actually, that's the only reason you are reading this book), it is time to break the walls of isolation and to cleanse your doubts and pain.

This is **AMONGST THE ALPHAS**.

May you find your power in the peace
of knowing what and who you really are

Dr. BAK NGUYEN

CHAPTER 1
"WHAT IS AN ALPHA?"
BY DR. BAK NGUYEN

I started the introduction of this book by telling you what we are not. We are not fighters, power hunger people nor compulsive gamblers who need to win at any cost. We do not look for a fight just for the pleasure of it. Actually, we do not take much pleasure in fighting.

> "To fight, to win, to achieve
> are three very different things."
> Dr. Bak Nguyen

Are Alphas the smartest, the strongest, the tallest? No, those are false and gross representations of ignorance. Not all Alphas are leaders or champions neither. To lead, to win, to do something extraordinary, one has to be an Alpha, but not all Alphas lead, win, or are extraordinary people.

An Alpha is a state of mind, a nature that is pushing for more, for better. Alpha means to come first, not by choice, but by nature. Alpha means to walk the miles and to open the roads.

We are all Alphas… somewhere in time. When we were amongst the apes, our ancestors were Alphas that adapted better and evolved into the dominant species. Amongst the animals, we are all Alphas… until we come neck to neck with a lion, a shark, or a snake…

So I guess, Alpha is relative. But then, individually, we are all the product of a race for life, at the time of our conception.

What were the odds that the spermatozoid carrying our genes make it through? 0.01% of chance of success!

into In other words, 99.9% of the spermatozoids never made it into Life. On that standard, we are at least 50% Alpha! This is great news! That means that we have the choice to activate or not those 50% of our genes, the **Alpha Gene**!

Is being an Alpha means to be a winner? I believe so, or else, we won't be alive to tell otherwise, just like those 99.9% of spermatozoids who swam with us and got lost in transition. We all have the gene of Life, the **Alpha Gene**.

So we are all fighters, grinders, and leaders of men? Not necessarily. Having a background in both biology and medicine, I can tell you that not everything in Life is about fighting and survival. The reason why those themes are so present is that those are the lyrics that resonate more to our ears.

It was about perception, not reality. Yes, a part of Life is about racing and fighting for survival, but that's only a little part of a bigger whole.

> "The bigger part of Life is about balance and harmony, living and dying, not just fighting to live nor dying to survive."
> Dr. Bak Nguyen

Once again, all the words were in that quote, only you will choose which resonate more to your ears: **Life**, **Balance**, **Harmony**, and Living or fighting, dying and surviving.

In the grand scheme of Life, from each death rose new lives, a different form of Life. To each loss, there is a gain, just somewhere else and of a different nature.

I guess, what I am trying to say is to have a broad perspective of the horizon, and you will see **balance**, **Life**, and **harmony**. Look too closely and with a narrow field of vision, and you are right, Life is about survival.

So is being an Alpha. Now that we know that we are from an Alpha Species, first amongst the Animals (if not, we won't be the dominant species), we still have to choose our place amongst our peers.

Being an Alpha usually means to be somehow stronger, better, bigger, smarter, wiser… but we all knew people with those trays who never fit the shoes.

So what is it about? Actually, we too often confuse Alphaness and leadership. Some Alphas aren't leaders, but all leaders are Alphas. The difference here is the choice we made when we face the crossroad, to embrace our **FEAR** or our **ALPHA GENE**.

So as I started, books ago, talking about entrepreneurship and leadership, saying that those cannot be learnt or trained into, but there are treads received from birth for us to nurture and to empower, I guess, I was… wrong.

Not all wrong, but partially wrong. Not everyone is an Alpha, a leader or an entrepreneur. Not everyone is a winner. But looking back at the origin of Life and our **ALPHA GENE**, there was a choice that we made somewhere, somehow.

For those of us that this will surprise, it is because others made the choice for us, and spent years following to reinforce that choice within us. And the alternative, well, that was to embrace **FEAR**.

So, just like the original sin for the Christians, we received from nature the **ALPHA GENE** as legacy. Conformity and Society replaced it with **FEAR** instead. Fear of what exactly?

Well, as a newborn, our mother protected us with all of her love. Her love transposed into the fear of us being hurt. Within days those who love us the most will be transferring their love and fear into us.

As we grew bigger and stronger, we will eventually be able to think for ourselves. That would be the perfect time to purge the fears. Unfortunately, the fear has mutated into an even greater fear.

By the time that we are strong enough to think for ourselves, the fear now is about being different and standing apart from all of them. If it doesn't make much sense to fear before, the fear of rejection is one that we know for being very real.

Then, Society doubled down on us, implementing doctrines and education as means to reinforce the beliefs started by our surroundings. You know the rest of the story.

So, to summarize the situation, we were born carrying the **ALPHA GENE**. Then, our parents and loved ones inoculated us with **FEAR** in the name of love and protection. Then, Society and Conformity doubled down on the culture of **FEAR** with education and doctrines.

Now, it will take much courage and work to overturn the trend and to stand on our own. To stand on our own means to stand apart from those we love and who love us. That's a hard decision, but unfortunately, it is one that we alone can make.

This is where most people back down facing the fence and the edge. Jumping that leap of faith is the journey to our destiny. No one talks about being an Alpha at this stage, but that first jump is the beginning of the awakening of our **ALPHA GENE**.

So when I said that being an Alpha is not for everyone, I was right. Where I was wrong is that everyone has the chance to become to be an Alpha, embracing their **ALPHA GENE**, but not everyone will make that choice.

And life is about choices, actions, and consequences, so once we chose, then, we will also have to deal with the consequences coming with it.

In other words, the longer one waits before embracing the **ALPHA GENE**, the longer he or she stays bathed in **FEAR**, the harder it will be to free him or herself from the fear. Not just because of the habits, but because of the pain of separation from those he or she grew up with.

That pain, I know all too well. Unfortunately, there is no other way. Being an Alpha is a choice that will draft a different course of Life, one with different outcomes, sacrifices, and purpose.

Once you embrace that **ALPHA GENE** of yours, you will start to see the world differently, with more layers, depth, and nuances. If you really want a clear answer out of me, being an Alpha is being free from the **FEAR** of the unknown, of the **FEAR** received from birth.

No two **ALPHAS** are alike, that's why they are Alphas. They will share common treads, but each Alpha is unique in his choices, his challenges, his destiny.

What is common to most **ALPHAS** are their difficulties and how the world reacts to them. On that, you can find many, many similitudes.

Being free from **FEAR**, the Alpha can see the problem for what it is without amplification nor emotions. The Alpha won't have the solution to most of the issues that he sees, but on one matter, the solution will appear clearly to him. That's when he will walk a path into the unknown, into the fog.

For the rest of the world, he is crazy and will fail for sure. To him, it was a none sense to stay behind looking at the fog and whispering fears and ignorances.

That person walking into the fog is the one we call crazy at first. Some will never return. But when they do, they become heroes, people we look up to. They've done the impossible, according to our standards.

If you ask them, you will hear how easy it was. They had some difficulties, sure, but it was a no brainer. This is when their fan-based will turned into hate. How can he say that it was easy when to us, it was impossible? And the inquisition will start. That's a classic.

So if there is one thing useful that you should take from this chapter is that once you have embraced your **ALPHA GENE**, make sure not to evaluate the world and your results using the same tools and standards as before.

As an **ALPHAS**, the tools and the rules are often not the same than those of the average. No, **ALPHAS** are not above the law, no one is. But under that line, there are worlds and layers, depth and perception.

> "Free from FEAR, that's the first wealth you will find, depth and nuances."
> Dr. Bak Nguyen

And you will react to that new perception of the world, of things. Seeing things under a new light, you will start thinking differently, then, will act upon your thoughts. Your actions will be consequential to your thoughts, and the consequences will be consequential to your actions.

And what is Life but an accumulation of consequences, and your reaction to them? Your path as an Alpha has started the day you free yourself from **FEAR**.

What you will become will follow your line of decisions. You may fail, you may succeed, your story will always be one of interest since you've tried something new, something unknown, something that might change the course of History.

History will retell the story of the one who will pass the finished line. That one is an Alpha, but so are the ones who pave the way to that victory. Many Alphas work in the dark and may have spent most of their lives to pave the way to the final victory.

History will not tell theirs stories, but they were the shoulders upon which we stand tall. We must keep honoring their memory, their courage, and boldness, leading the way through the unknown.

Not all Alphas are recognized. Those who are, are merely the tip of the iceberg. I started this book by saying that not everyone is an Alpha. I stand by that point. Already, after a chapter, we know that everyone alive has an **ALPHA GENE**.

From there, we chose or not to express that gene, to embrace that part of our nature. The Alphas aren't just those figures we know as heroes or leaders, they are everywhere, leading the charge on their terms, their way.

We are a nation of Alphas, we only need to decide to be so and to expand our horizon and our grasp.
This is **AMONGST THE ALPHAS**.

May you find your power in the peace
of knowing what and who you really are.

Dr. BAK NGUYEN

CHAPTER 2
"HOW DO ALPHAS RECOGNIZE EACH OTHER?"
BY DR. BAK NGUYEN

Common belief will lead us to think that as soon as two Alphas are in the same room, they will fight until one is dead. Well, again, this is the minority and the folkloric tales. Yes, some will be fighting, but most of the time, they will go their separate ways.

Please do not confuse those hungry of power with the Alphas. Yes, some hungry power people will do everything they can think of to keep power. They are Alphas, but they do not represent the Alpha Species.

As most Alphas have their own goal and challenges in life, most will choose the easiest path to stay on course. That often means to avoid conflict, unless their goal was power itself. So forget the image of the 2 gorillas fighting to the death to know who is the Alpha. This is a fraction of truth and a distortion of reality.

> "Amongst people, we try to connect. Amongst peers, it is simply too hard to resist, once we connected, then we start to compare."
> Dr. Bak Nguyen

This is not only a truth amongst Alphas but amongst any gathering of people, brotherhood, organization. Once we connect, then we start to compare. To understand the difference, one can feel it in the air.

Every time a new connection is made, the energy is going up. Both parties will feel it. Our own biology will be responding to the encounter, liberating bonding and social chemicals, **oxytocin**. That's a feel-good hormone, almost instantly, we will feel good and be drawn to the feeling and the connection.

At this stage, what we are looking to do is to keep the connection going, keeping the flow of hormones coming. We are seeking all the similarities that would bind us together. Even the differences, we find interesting. We are connecting. We are learning to know and to accept each other.

But after a while, the novelty effect is wearing off, and most of the similarities are now deeply entrenched. We see the other person now as a mirror more than a unique soul, a mirror of ourselves.

Since life is nothing but dynamic, things are evolving and moving. To keep the same connection, both people, from the mirror relationship, should be moving at the same pace, in the same direction.

It is only a question of time before either the pace or the direction will diverse. We are all free to choose and to change, aren't we? Well, this is where the conflict will happen. From the wearing off of the novelty effect, this is fewer and fewer hormones flowing from the relationship. That's craving both our mind and body.

Now, add on top of it, the shifting of the mirror and its subject. From living both their individual lives, that special bond formed is slowly bending. From the mirror, the reflection is bending in all directions. What we saw as similitudes before aren't similitude. What looked perfect before is now distorted and asymmetrical. The flaws are coming out. Who's flaws are we seeing?

This is just the effect of time on a relationship. Now add on top of it that one of the parties is evolving faster than the other. The blend and deformation are happening even at a greater scale and a faster pace. Panic will enter the system.

Looking in that mirror, we will undoubtedly feel unease and insecure. That reflection was an image of us that we like. Now that the image is changing faster and differently than we like, we notice that we are not in control of that reflection. Actually, we will feel sick at our core, just like our identity was under attack.

The connection will break, freeing the illusion and the hormones. What was once a beautiful sensation to have found a perfect reflection of ourselves is now the reminder of everything that we are not, of everything that we lack. We are feeling left behind, betrayed. We may be left behind, but betrayed? Really?

> "One always sees what
> one chooses to see, nothing else."
> Dr. Bak Nguyen

If we could keep that in mind, we would be so much wiser. We would understand that from the beginning, both parties were projecting something they like at each other. Because of the similarities, the illusion of reflection was possible. It wasn't just a reflection, but an improved one since we could ignore the flaws and amplify the traits that we loved.

Don't get me wrong, we all do it. Actually, it is one of the best and fastest ways to evolve, to find people to connect with in order to have a reflection on which we could judge ourselves. The keyword here is to judge ourselves, not the other party.

> "Judging is painful."
> Dr. Bak Nguyen

But since we aren't all wise creatures, we do not judge ourselves since we lack the courage and the intention. So as a reaction by default, we will judge the other party instead. We all do.

In the beginning, that judgemental look showed the similarities and the admiration's traits. We were just too happy to seek a genuine connection and to make it last. Not just because of the reflection, but because that made us feel bigger, connecting with another person whom we seek osmosis with.

That's what is going through all minds, by connecting with someone. Somehow, our minds think that everything accessible to them is now also available to us. That was never said or part of any deal, but that's how we lied to ourselves.

The lies were so real that the body even reacted, doubling down of the feel-good effect with the release of even more hormones. This is what is causing a distorted perception of reality. Distorted, maybe, but one that makes us feel so good that it is hard to not seek for more.

Sounds crazy? Well, this is how friendships are born. The only difference between a real friendship that will last longer is how mutual is that reaction, that chemical reaction to a distorted reality.

Well, that is not true, at least, not completely. In the matter of friendship, the bond could be a genuine one if there was an external factor that united the two parties, a common enemy, a shared problem, a common goal.

If that's the case, for as long as the common external factor is present, the bond will be real and not distorted. But as soon as that enemy is defeated, as the problem is solved or has expired, as the goal is achieved, then, the relationship will redefine itself, even without the parties noticing.

Unless there is another common challenge or enemy, the celebration will last for a short while, and the joy will fade into souvenirs. Much sooner than expected, those same souvenirs will grow into burdens if not purged.

When I said that both parties needed to move at the same pace and in the same direction, after the disappearance of the common cause binding the parties, it becomes inevitable for each party to go on a different path, one of their choosing, and at their own pace.

On paper, that makes much sense, and both parties will have shared great and memorable moments together. Unless both move on at the same pace and at the same time, one will now feel left behind by the other (moving on).

Instead of moving on him or herself, that one left behind will start blaming the other for the unease feeling of having to walk a new journey, alone. This is how old friendships sometimes, grow into bitterness and jealousy. Be warned.

This was in the event that there was something genuine uniting the parties. Nowadays, we are enjoying peace and prosperity, maybe not abundance, but prosperity for sure. Nowadays, most of our encounters happen on a social basis, often without real threat and common enemy.

The initial bond will feel the same, but the comparison and the jealousy are much more inclined to happen… faster than we could see it coming.

When you see someone in the room, and you simply hate that person without any good reason, what do you think happened inside your head? You projected yourself within a relationship with that person and went through all of the steps described above.

Since, very few can unite you, the feeling of rejection will take over and make you feel unease to the point of hating that person who left you behind. You haven't even asked his name yet…

That's the only way to explain why the feeling was so visceral and true, even before the first exchange of words. Remember that it was all about you, not the other party.

> "Good or bad, most relationships are about us and our perception, not about the other party."
> **Dr. Bak Nguyen**

Well, this is exactly what is happening every single time that one meets with an Alpha. Sometimes the connection, but most of the time, the hate and animosity. For most Alphas, they will be hurt by the reactions. If that does not kill them and their spirit, they will grow, sooner or later to accept the sad truth: not to expect much from social interactions.

That's how most Alphas will go their way, independent and distant. They aren't bad people nor insensitive either, they just moved on from the unnecessary pain and drama. They are the independent thinkers and free spirits often found in artists and inventors.

Some will care about others, even if they are rejected because of their difference, their Alpha Gene. They will act in the common interest because they can. These Alphas, unless they are protected, will eventually grow their influence to have a team of people protecting them from the crowd until the comparison appears inside of their own team and they will have to run to the crowd for protection.

I just described to you the blueprint of power. And authority? Well, an Alpha is someone free of **FEAR**. An Alpha can also turn away from his **ALPHA GENE** and embrace **FEAR** eventually. If that Alpha is in a position of power, the **FEAR** of losing power will drift his mindset from **ALPHA** to **FEAR**.

This is how and why he will encourage the creation of authority to maintain his power and influence. That's the corruption that **FEAR** will have over, not just **ALPHAS**, but all those stuck at the same place, power or not.

> "Stillness and stiffness will create authority.
> This has nothing to do with Alphaness."
> Dr. Bak Nguyen

So what happens when two Alphas meet? As I said at the beginning of this chapter, it does rarely end in those battle to the death kind of situation. You see, in reality, most Alphas aren't leaders nor have many followers.

Especially in today's reality where the cult of individualist is to its apogee, most Alphas are isolated, alone. Being different and alone, these Alphas have spent much of their lives craving for genuine connections, simply to have someone to share with.

Well, what do you think will happen when two Alphas meet? They connect, right away, they were craving for that! Usually, social popularity has nothing to do with the real nature of an Alpha. Real and genuine Alpha aren't always on the front line and taking pictures.

Most of the Alphas are very discreet people… until you ask the right question and the light comes out naturally. So as it is easy to spot who is the most popular person in a crowd, to spot the Alphas is not as easy.

Once again, do not twist my words, that most popular person may also be an Alpha, but he or she isn't representative of most Alphas. So no, rarely, the other Alphas will be drawn based solely on popularity.

I have to remain you that most Alphas are busy walking their unique path. So unless the encounter will bear any interest for their own quest, most Alphas aren't inclined to spend time connecting with popularity.

They do not have time either to judge or to be jealous. They are not above that, they are simply too busy to care. Those are the traits that another Alpha will notice.

When 2 Alphas get together, they talk about experiences and ideas, not who they are. That's why even if they might have big egos and personalities, rarely 2 Alphas will collide. Unless one is actively and willingly stepping on the toes of the other, if they disagree, they will enjoy the conversation, but won't connect further.

If they agree, they will spend a wonderful time exchanging. Most of the time, Alphas are isolated as independent and different thinkers, just to have someone vibrating on the same frequency is enough to initiate a friendship and a genuine conversation.

Genuine, that's something else that **Alphas** will be seeking actively. Small talks, social talks, even popularity bear little interest to Alphas. An **Alpha** is someone who purged their **FEAR**, so most **Alphas** are less insecure and much more open to share, as long as it is genuine.

Do you want a simple example? Let replace Alphas with a trendy contemporary term, entrepreneurs. Well, not all entrepreneurs are leaders. Not all entrepreneurs are popular, but all entrepreneurs mind their business and are dedicated to its success. You can clearly see the portrait.

So replace **ENTREPRENEUR** with **ALPHA**, and you will get the picture. Now, are all entrepreneurs Alphas? I am not sure, but to create something new, to go against the odds, and to embrace the risks of the unknown, these are usually what an Alpha will do.

> "Alphaness is not as status,
> it is a choice and a state of mind."
> Dr. Bak Nguyen

On the matter, I will push even further. Most Alphas are in a quest. Most Alphas crave for a genuine conversation and some company (for as long as they aren't diverting from their path). So most Alphas will welcome the genuine friendship.

Since Alphas can be found in all the classes and ages of Society, when two Alphas of different ages meet, one might become the mentor of the other.

When they are from very different fields, great friendship shall appear. When they are in the same field, either they will join force or become rivals. Either way, respect is well established.

So very rarely, you will assist to that dual to the death of two Alphas. The Alphas are usually not in a crowd. They are busy walking their own path. When they connect, they are looking for genuine. And above all, they hate to waste time! That's how they recognize one another.

This is **AMONGST THE ALPHAS**.

Dr. BAK NGUYEN

CHAPTER 3
"HOW DO YOU DEAL WITH ALPHAS?"
BY DR. BAK NGUYEN

An Alpha rarely moves forward out of pride, courage, or conviction. If an Alpha is stepping forward, it is because he or she feels something real, something genuine that he or she can touch while no one else can even sense.

> "An Alpha is no gambler, even if the Alpha is a pretty darn good player."
> Dr. Bak Nguyen

On that matter, an Alpha is looking for leverage as he moves forward. He has the insurance that what he sees is real and can be done, that's his conviction.

On the way, he will be dealing with people, he might be trading for leverage to speed up his way to achievement, but he will not compromise, ever.

Those who do not understand the nature of Alphas often think that they are compromising. They are not. They trade what they deem acceptable to reach their goal. They **trade**, they do not compromise. In that sense, Alphas are masters of the art of prioritizing.

An Alpha might look like a gambler to the rest of the world since no one sees what he sees. Ask him, and it was a safe bet, the views were clear and the thinking rational. An Alpha is not a gambler. He might be a pretty good player, though.

Alphas do not negotiate, they get things done. If that means that they have to deal, so yes, they deal, but they will always have out of that deal what is the most valuable to their eyes. Some will drive a hard bargain, others will be more easy going, the style is more about their training and personal experience.

>"Not all heroes are Alphas."
>Dr. Bak Nguyen

We all saw these movies where the courageous hero is saving the day, giving his life in the trade. We love these kinds of characters. Well, the act may be heroic, but that wasn't an Alpha's attitude at his core. To be courageous, one has to acknowledge his **FEAR** and grow beyond it.

Well, most Alphas started with purging their fear… so courage is not something that should matter much in the balance. I am not saying that Alphas do not fear, but most of the lives, they are dumping their fear one after the next.

>"Unlike the rest of the world,
>you can't define an Alpha through his fear."
>Dr. Bak Nguyen

Fear, not weakness. Even if an Alpha is less burden by fears, he is like anyone else, he still has flaws to address. Once again, the thinking is different.

For Alphas, to address their flaws is not a priority. Throughout their journey, they will have the opportunity to learn something that will help level their flaws, or they might simply find ways to avoid them.

> "Alphas do not believe in perfection, they believe in results."
> Dr. Bak Nguyen

Look at all the over-achievers, are they looking to reach perfection? They are looking to have things work and to implement their idea, their solution. They are often as naive as children discovering a new way to do things. They will do it, and as it works, they will move on. That's in their nature.

One thing that will characterize all Alphas is that none of them are transactional. They shake hands and make deals, but it is always about the journey and the relationship, not the transaction.

You see, for an Alpha, there is one thing that matters to him or her more than the deal itself: to keep moving forward in his or her personal quest. That being said, most Alphas are very **self-aware** and will need to feel something genuine out of each deal.

While most people are looking for a pure win, the Alphas are looking for more, for better. Each Alpha needs to feel that they are growing from each deal, each step, that they've learnt something new.

On the matter, what is the difference between an Alpha and an arrogant person? Both know the existence of their **ALPHA GENE**, so why is one so different than the other?

The main difference stands in the fact that the arrogant person put him or herself in the center of the equation. He is doing things for himself. They may have embraced the **ALPHA GENE**, but their impact is limited to who and what there are.

The **ALPHAS** we are noticing more, those achieving the impossible, those drafting and building the world of tomorrow have chosen a singly different path. They removed themselves from the center of the equation and are serving purposes bigger than themselves.

By doing so, they will grow a big as the issues they are addressing… if they do not die on the way. It is like a fish, ever heard of the saying that a fish will grow as big as its pond? What will define the power and impact of an Alpha is the size of their spirit, their minds, and their heart.

For that reason, when you shake hands with an Alpha and seal a deal, that person will be looking at the future, more than just about the profit.

> "For Alphas, bigger is not necessarily better.
> To get things done swiftly is."
> Dr. Bak Nguyen

So as "**wannabe**" will be looking to score as big as possible, the Alphas will concentrate their effort on the impact they can do in a given situation. If they do not see how they can be of help, they might simply move on.

So again, those courageous leaders that fought through hell and back, those are the folklores of legends, not the reality of the Alphas.

So an Alpha can be anyone who decided to embrace their **ALPHA GENE**, started to purge their **FEARS**, and is looking for his or her worth. That's the genesis.

From there, the Alpha will gain much strength and power as he or she gains in security and build up his or her confidence to the point of removing him or herself from the center of the equation. As they are freeing their potential from the boundaries of themselves (perspective and horizon), they are learning and mastering while doing.

An Alpha can be anyone you meet on the street. You might feel a certain presence, but until you shake their hands and see them in action, it is hard to distinguish the Alphas from the others, the arrogant, and the wannabe. And the main reason is that they all started from the same point, embracing their **ALPHA GENE**.

The wanna be just started his journey. The arrogant has started dropping his **FEAR** but is still insecure about looking up, expanding his horizon from his bellybutton. The Alpha got through these phases and has grown enough to look up and removing himself from the center of his attention.

How should you deal with any of them? With respect. If you know that someday, you too will be phasing through these steps, see the wannabe as a child learning to walk.

See the arrogant as a teenager testing the boundaries looking for him or herself, and the Alpha as the mature phase of one ready to give. Be kind, since you are looking at a mirror of a possible future.

Unfortunately, most people do not see the future. They discard it as fiction. They are so insecure that they close themselves up to the limit of having a hard time breathing.

They will hardly see the present. The only two things they are good at is to talk about the past with their bellybutton blocking most of the field of vision.

In other words, we crucify the *wannabe*, we hate and are doing our best to take down the *arrogant* (that's a little harder since those are usually strong players). Those are the people that might lift us you one day, if we haven't killed them before!

And the crowd will bear the weight of their sins. Since the **ALPHA GENE** is in all of us, what you do think we are all learning? We are adding more and more filters and fear of our chances of coming out and embracing our own **ALPHA GENE**.

> "Alpha is a state of mind and a choice."
> Dr. Bak Nguyen

Knowing this, how do you deal with an Alpha? You treat him or her as you would anyone else. Most of the time, you won't even notice the difference. They will play the game of negotiation, they will reinforce their point, and they will compromise.

Some will be kind and gentle, others will be aggressive and without pity. Being an Alpha is to be fear-free, and laser-focused on their goal, not to be nice or not.

Alphas are also secure people. They might have a negotiating style that they like, but they do not humiliate people for the pleasure of it. In other words, Alphas will not strip you down from a deal just to feel bigger. They do not need that, they don't have time for that.

Those who are leveraging on fear and intimidation are often insecure people, not Alphas. Unfortunately, those tactics of fear and intimidation work, so not all winners are Alphas…

Can you have the upper hand negotiating with an Alpha? If you know what you want, and that isn't the main interest of the Alpha, you could end up with your most successful negotiation. But Alphas, rarely give up what they seek. One way or another, they will get what they want.

> "An Alpha is a state of mind,
> not a tactic nor a strategy."
> Dr. Bak Nguyen

Please do not confuse those with the **ALPHA GENE**. Alphaness is about who they are and what they want, not how they make it happen. So there is no special secret to come up on top of dealing with Alphas.

You must know who you are and what you want, then, trade with them. On the other hand, dealing with Alphas, you may have a very strong upside as a side effect.

Notice their confidence and their focus, feel their drive and determination, that might inspire you to jump-start your own journey, embracing your **ALPHA GENE**.

In all the stories, of any kind, there is always that part where one has to look for his destiny. Well, it is always the same story over and over again, only for the first time, with a new face embracing his or her **ALPHA GENE**.

That's you win, look at **ALPHAS** as your future, an example of what to come. Get inspiration from what you feel in their presence and, as you are ready, follow your heart.

Your heart, not your head! Your head is recording the event and the past. It is making sense of all the recorded data and is trying to sort and filter them into libraries and connections. There is nothing about predicting the future there.

Only your heart can aspire for what will come next, for something new, something different. Your heart will feel what can be, and it will act as such.

And about your spirit? You will need your spirit to keep believing in the way to achieve what you felt. This is how we are drafting and building the future. The head, well, the head eventually will join in and will help with the HOW.

Knowing the recipe is not enough. One still needs to see it in action first. This is what you are gaining each time you are in proximity and dealing with an Alpha, to understand how he or she is drafting the future right in front of your eyes.

What to you was a simple transaction is to him a bridge crossed or built, a step closer to completion. Do not look at what he is doing nor try to understand his logic, that won't help you.

Look at how he managed to keep his drive up, how he managed to convince you of joining his point of view, and what you felt doing so. Vibe at his confidence and his determination, that's the common trait that can be transferred.

> "Catch the ALPHA's enthusiasm and vibe and, as you are ready, start your own journey."
> Dr. Bak Nguyen

What is interesting is how 2 alphas may deal with one another. Yes, there is that thin possibility that they might fight, but it is more a story for the silver screen than real life (their time is too valuable for them to fight, and that, they are very well aware of). Most of the time, they will dance throughout their encounter.

The first thing that they will measure is the strength and intention of the other party. They will show respect, but won't kneel down. They will poke and test the other party to probe their depth and intelligence.

Now, remember that most Alphas are focused on their goal, depending on their state of mind at the time of the encounter, they might be open or not to connect. Alphas aren't people who crave for connection.

The magic some times happen when two Alphas of different age come in contact. As the older one recognize an Alpha in the becoming, often, he will project himself in the younger mind.

Some will nurture one from the wannabe phase, some, from the arrogant phase. Some others will see something not expressed yet and try to awake the **ALPHA GENE**.

I have different mentors landing me their hand at each stage of my evolution. The encounters are often the same, we meet within a conversation or the execution of a task, and magic kicks in.

At the primary stages, **Pride** is often the obstacle to a genuine relationship. Pride and Control. Well, if I really think of it, I can summarize it with **Insecurity**. The more insecure a protege is, the harder he or she is to be mentored.

Mentors are not all **ALPHAS** either. Some are, some have stopped their evolution somewhere on the path. No matter the stage of each party, the shock and friction always come from insecurity.

> "Pride is to protect with all of yourself,
> your vulnerabilities."
> Dr. Bak Nguyen

In my experiences, my regrets are to have met great and generous minds trying to help me when I wasn't ready to listen and to open up yet. The day that all changed is the day when I accepted my flaws and stopped focussing on them.

I told you that an Alpha is someone who is purging his fear, one after the next. Well, one of the common fear of everyone is to have other pointing out their flaws and weaknesses. Most of us spend our entire life trying to either hide those flaws or erasing them.

I was too busy betting on my strength and discovering my powers as an Alpha to be slowed down by my weaknesses and flaws. For long, I heard the saying that one can go only as far as his weakness will allow. Well, what I can tell you is that there is a world between that limits and where you stand right now.

I ran those miles, each day, day after day. The limits, I still have, but running fast, I leave many things behind, the unnecessary weight. I often have to leave a great part of my personal story, my successes, my strengths in order to gain more and more speed.

Then it hit me: if I am discarding great assets because they do not serve me anymore, why do I keep bearing my flaws all the way through? Running the miles day after day was hard enough, why do I have to carry extra weight.

So I purged most of my flaws and weaknesses, leaving them behind. That worked pretty well for a little while until I couldn't cut anything else. Funny thing, flaws, and weaknesses are something dearest part of yourself.

But guess what? I had fewer flaws to deal with since the daily purges. I had less to deal with and so much energy and power coming from my runs, faster and faster.

It took me years to arrive at that stage, but my encounters and friendship with other Alphas and mentors got me to the point of liberation, freeing myself not only of fears but also of flaws.

And for what was left to solve, I address them with more knowledge, power, and confidence. Actually, that's not completely true, I address them only if I need and when I do. I have more **knowledge, power** and **confidence**.

"Craving for control is the best patch of insecurity."
Dr. Bak Nguyen

On the same line of thoughts, gaining in speed and power, I lighten myself with more and more ease, dropping the flaws and addressing those too close to drop. Well, the main advantage was that my confidence grew to the point of eclipsing most of my insecurities.

I still don't know what will come, but I have a pretty good idea. I still can't predict when it will happen, but I know it will. It is with this confidence that I face the truth and the reflection looking back at me, from the eyes of my mentors.

Well, because I was purging my fears, my flaws, and my insecurities, I also let go of my need for control. When I talk about looking at our bellybutton, the real term I should have used, is trying to keep control over everything.

The day I let go of control, I started to react more freely to the world and to the events. Because I see so much more than myself, it is so much more interesting to address the needs of the world instead of my own. Does that make any sense to you?

Let me clarify and reformulate. Because I now see the world, I see its flaws. It is so much easier and less painful to address those flaws than to address my own. And each time I solve a problem, I grow both my **knowledge** and **confidence**.

What a great recipe, don't you agree? Well, it all started with me embracing the **ALPHA GENE**. It took me much time, but as I met with other Alphas and observed them, I mimicked their attitude and started on my own path.

The more I was running, the more I could feel their vibe and understand their secrets. This whole chapter was about interacting with **ALPHAS**.

Well, you meet them every day. You talk to them, you judge them, you may even laugh at them. Start feeling what it's like to be in their shoes and feel their vibe.

Sooner than you think, you will be on your way to becoming one. Not all wannabe will grow into Alphas. Not all arrogant with leave their pride behind and look up the path of the Alphas. Is it destiny? I prefer to think that it was a matter of being open to learn and to keep dropping the weights and the unnecessary.

What are you carrying extra all day long?

This is **AMONGST THE ALPHAS**.

May you find your power in the peace
of knowing what and who you really are.

Dr. BAK NGUYEN

CHAPTER 4
"ARE ALPHAS PROTECTORS?"
BY DR. BAK NGUYEN

I told you already that to grow in power and knowledge, an Alpha has to spread his wings and to fly, higher and higher. To do so, he has to outgrow his boundaries and body.

The only effective way to do so is to start caring about issues that are bigger than themselves. This is not only sounding great, it is also very true! But the real key behind this logic is that to grow, the Alphas (just like anyone else) have to cut down the weights and the burdens.

Weights and burdens are often synonyms to liabilities. Easy enough to follow until that point. But what is a liability? Spend a few minutes to ask yourself what is a liability and what are yours.

Let's borrow from Robert Kiyosaki, best-selling author and educator, his definition of liability: a liability is what will eat you, in opposition to an asset which is feeding us!

The picture is clear enough, who would ever want something eating us? Well, we all have liabilities, what are yours? Go on, say it!

Those liabilities are all people and things dear to our hearts. So now, the real picture is painted, can we cut people and things dear to us?

Well, for Alphas, to apply themselves solving bigger issues, issues of other people, they gain the opportunity to evolve without pain, since it won't be their liabilities that they will be cutting, but someone else's!

The catch is that if they did not have any experience cutting their own, they would never have enough power and influence to cut those of others. Don't get me wrong, it is much harder to cut down other people's liabilities than our own. More difficult, yes, but also painless!

The first time I really tried that mentality was a few years ago when my mentor asked me to take care of a matter of public health on a national scope. It wasn't my cup to drink nor my field of expertise, but they were desperate and needed help.

To be frank, I had already so much on my shoulders that I was about to move on, when he told me to address that particular issue. To cut all resistance, he told me that it was an exercise, nothing more and nothing less.

The man is a real genius. With the word **exercise**, it wasn't about my Identity anymore. I dropped both the question and the resistance, and I put myself to work.

Well, within 3 months, a few meetings, some phone calls, and a few emails, I set up the table for the major actors and the decision-makers to solve the crisis. Me, an outsider!

I had nothing to gain acting in that field. I had nothing to lose either, but my time and energy. I grew much from the journey.

My confidence built up exponentially, my knowledge expanded, but something new also appeared: my influence.

Taking care of issues much bigger than myself, I outgrew most of the boundaries that were holding me down: my **Identity**! I dropped the questions for 3 months. When I came back, some of those questions were now obsolete, and the remaining were not as heavy to bear anymore.

I push my mind and my spirit in the service of others, and my influence appeared and grew. It has never stopped growing since.

That day, I've learnt a great lesson of life, to stop limiting myself to me! I put aside the **question of Identity**, and apply my energy to solve other's people's problems, those I could see an angle, a way to leverage.

I wasn't too alien to the concept. You call me doctor because I spent half of my life treating people as a dentist. Well, this is pretty similar, but instead of serving people with my surgical skills, I am serving society with my entire being.

A few years later, I reset myself completely dropping what was left of the burdens, the insecurities, and the flaws, opening myself up to the world. I maintain the **YESMAN'S** challenge for 18 months, saying yes to almost every opportunity.

That took care of most of the remaining burdens. Today, I still have flaws and liabilities, but I'm also pretty good at the art of cutting off the extra weight.

Because I did it on myself first, I am capable of repeating the procedure on others. Because I know the pain coming with it, I am holding the surgical tools with security, with the insurance that good and better will come.

And the only way one can have the strength to go through this, again and again, is with kindness and hope. So yes, Alphas are protectors.

Until they reach their maturity, wannabe and arrogant will still be looking at themselves to define the world and their actions. But as soon as they are secure enough to take their eyes off of their bellybutton, and to put someone else at the center of their attention, they will grow soon enough.

And the growth? It is intoxicating! Once you've tasted such energy, such power, such humanity, you just want more! You want to matter more, you want to help more, you want to make the world a better place!

> "Sharing is the way to grow."
> Dr. Bak Nguyen

On a smaller scale, why would an Alpha take someone under his or her wing? For the company, of course, but also because the same logic will apply. To mentor a younger mind with potential is to have the chance to live once more, wiser, and with fewer pains!

I had the privilege to have many mentors in my life. I also mentored many people. I can tell you that the mentor grows as much, if not more than the protege that he or she is training.

> "The recipe is always the same: less pain, less identity, less pride, more results."
> Dr. Bak Nguyen

So are Alphas and mentors teaching from the goodness of their heart? I think that they are teaching from cleverness: they found a way to grow their heart while growing in power, knowledge, and influence. And they achieved all of it from being generous and kind! What a great deal!

We are all fundamentally selfish and self-centred; that's in our genes. How to outgrow that part since we can simply carve it out? The **ALPHA'S WAY**, evolving and growing without the pain of amputation while serving others!

So yes, an Alpha will help you if he or she knows how. Yes, even if you have much to gain out of the relationship and haven't given much in return, the Alpha will still grow much from his or her interaction helping you.

Unless you are an Alpha yourself, he helped because he could, not just because he cared, and not because it was about you! But if you are an Alpha and showing potential, you might catch their eyes and poke their interests.

Some will show interest and offer to nurture you, to mentor you. Don't be mistaken, you will be doing the hard work and sharing the fruit of your labor, and that will be the best deal you ever took in your life!

To the question, is an Alpha a protector? I think it is a trait of character that most Alphas have. Alphas are more about empowerment and liberations than about protecting.

To protect is to keep someone from harm. There are many ways to achieve that goal. Well, Alphas will prepare their protege to face the challenge without blinking. They will get hurt, they just need to know how to heal and to deal with the pain.

And to us all, what will an Alpha do? He or she might serve us in the name of the greater good, taking care of matters we don't even know existed.

Some will do it from the goodness of their heart, some will out of the leverage of the **ALPHA'S WAY**, but all Alphas will help with their unique skills and perspective.

> "No matter the intentions, Alphas will be aiming for results. Judge them on the results, not the intentions."
> Dr. Bak Nguyen

It is simply too easy to admire those with good intentions. Unfortunately, that is neither the beginning nor is it enough. As a society, we have to stop lying to each other and to ourselves thinking that good intentions, pure purpose, and to give it our best is enough.

It is to be committed, to push for results, and to keep going through that will keep us at the peak of evolution, as the dominant species.

To have is the beginning. To leave it behind is the next lesson in order to be… bigger, better, wiser. We are all Alphas inside, only you can decide where you will stand!

So be kind, be respectful and land a hand, just because you could. Find ways to do so without diverting from your own race, and you will have found a way to speed up **Momentum** and **acceleration**.

This is **AMONGST THE ALPHAS**.

May you find your power in the peace
of knowing what and who you really are.

Dr. BAK NGUYEN

CHAPTER 5
"WHAT DO ALPHAS SACRIFICE?"
BY DR. BAK NGUYEN

I am not sure that sacrifice is the right word here. Sure being an Alpha, you are different, and you tend to like different things.

A little earlier, my assistant asked me about my social life. She asked me why even if I seem to have many friends and have the ability to forge new friendships easily, why don't I hang out more often with my friends?

Is that a sacrifice? My answer to her was unexpected. As an overachiever, I am committed to keep achieving, more and faster, better and broader. I do open up to many people and have many great exchanges and conversations on a daily basis, but I do not crave for them, nor do I seek them actively.

In my function as a dentist, I meet with people. I work with people, I serve people. Every time, I give it my best, my all, hoping to connect with every person I meet genuinely.

Some, I will enjoy more the company, others, well, I will stay polite and do my job. But since I cleared out most of my insecurities, I do not draw my identity from the opinions of others anymore.

So when I connect, it is to share something new, something genuine, not to see my reflection in the conversation. I really believe that most people need the psychological support of their peers and friends to remind them of who they are. I don't, not anymore.

On the contrary, being an Alpha, I was so many times burned and hurt by the judgment of those I considered friends and family. Now I know, it isn't about me, it was about them and their insecurities.

It took me nearly 40 years to finally understand the dynamics of social interaction and relationship being an alpha, but now, I know. And since I know what might come out of those kinds of conversations, why would I seek them?

That's how I do not seek gathering nor social talks. On the other hand, I welcome new and genuine connections. For as long as the conversation is toward connecting and sharing, I am the first one there and the last one leaving.

I will also be present if my help is required. Once again, it is not about a person but about how I can help. Actions and Results more than words and intentions.

Would you consider this to be a sacrifice? In a sense, I accepted a long time ago that embracing my **ALPHA GENE**, I will be cutting myself from many of my friends and family who are comfortably set in the average.

Did that hurt? I would lie if I said that I was fine from the wounds and the scars. But I tried the alternative, to stay behind and to try to fit in.

I did that for nearly 35 years and guess what? It didn't change what needed to come. I was miserable, and those people I tried to please were still not happy, and they ended up stepping all over me. I was hurt, but I survived. I healed, and now I am free on my way to my destiny.

If I had to do it all over again, would I change anything? I would spare myself the years of waiting and misery, knowing that the conclusion would be the same.

Is that a sacrifice to walk out from people we love and grew up with? Trust me, I did not walk out, I got kicked out. So why the suffering while waiting for the fatal moment to happen?

I learn a precious lesson out of that: to be true to myself and to live without regret. For years I denied myself my true calling and identity. I did that to please people that weren't either happy, either content. So why the pain?

To you, I can't save you from the unavoidable choice you will have to make as you'll embrace your **ALPHA GENE**: to be different, to be rejected. Is that a sacrifice?

> "Sacrifice is a word of those victims of the world, not those drafting it."
> Dr. Bak Nguyen

You just need to be aware of what will come, undeniably, and what consequences your choice will have. Be warned and have no regret. Once you know and make up your mind, throw your doubts away, you need your energy for much more important things.

> "The price to being different will eventually be your best deal if you keep pushing."
> Dr. Bak Nguyen

The choice was not to love or not but to be or not. And I try not to be, it does not work! My advice, be grateful, be graceful, and be yourself. Be kind and do not step over people, and take your rightful place in the world.

We all have a 50/50 chance to be an Alpha, if we chose so. Looking at my own personal story, I will add that some of us are more inclined than others to embrace the **ALPHA GENE**.

One thing for sure, this gene is not hereditary, everyone received it from the concept of Life itself. It's okay if you are not cut for it, the goal of life is to find your happiness, yours! Make up your mind and be happy, without second guess nor regret.

For those of you who embraced the **ALPHA GENE** or are thinking of doing so, do it knowing what will come out of your choice. It is no sacrifice, it is part of the game. The price will be paid, but if you are not prepared, you might overpay!

> "Alpha is another game with other rules,
> players, and gravity."
> Dr. Bak Nguyen

One of the other sacrifices concerning the Alphas, is that they will have to unlearn most of what they learn from society and Conformity since **ALPHA** is another game with other rules, players, and gravity.

One of the worse mistakes one can make is to judge and evaluate his progression as an Alpha from the old tools given to the average. The game is not the same, the ground has shifted, you must leave the old behind and be ready to embrace the new.

This actually is one of the hardest steps to take on your way being an Alpha, to leave your reference system and values behind.

Take the example of being rejected by most of your family and friends. This is a sacrifice and much of a price based on your previous values.

But as an Alpha, you know that you have a purpose and you owe it to yourself and to God to discover what you are made of. What was the sacrifice? To sit on your God-given potential or to leave the expectations and your loved ones behind?

You see, for as long as you are still talking about sacrifice, you are still very attached to the average value system. It is okay, but you are not doing yourself any favor since you'll be second-guessing your decisions and actions every step of the way.

I did not have to bear that doubt since I stuck with them for as long as I could... but the pain, I bear twice! Now, I don't need the pain on top of it! Make up your mind and have the right mindset and value system.

Even better, limit your value system to the minimum, it will increase your energy. For those of you interested in that matter, **THE ENERGY FORMULA**, my 53rd book will cover in details on how to increase your energy.

> "Alpha or not, the key to growth is to stay as open as possible. Take in, digest, and give back. Then repeat."
> Dr. Bak Nguyen

Is taking in a sacrifice? Is digesting a sacrifice? Is giving back a sacrifice? Is repeating a sacrifice? Stop torturing yourself with the words and labels, and just do what you must, what you feel, what will make you happy.

> "Make leverage of each of your liabilities,
> and you will always be moving forward."
> Dr. Bak Nguyen

Those are the words of an Alpha, one free of fears, of insecurities, and of burden. I still have many responsibilities, I have grateful to have people counting on me for results. I still have flaws to address, I am happy to have things to leverage on… the day I will understand how to use them.

I am grateful to be alive and to have an opportunity to give back, to play my part. From the moment I accepted that, I found happiness. I am happy ever since, happy, but never content.

To me each day is a new day, a new adventure and new stories to discover and to tell, new people to meet, and new pleasure to have.

If I meet with my old friends, I am glad, if I don't, it's no big deal. To walk my path and I share along the way. I won't stop to share, but I will share along the way. You are benefitting from that sharing at this exact moment.

Some will say that this is my curse to keep moving forward until I die. Well, to me, it is no sacrifice, it is a privilege.

> "The day that I won't be able to move forward,
> I've died a year earlier!"
> Dr. Bak Nguyen

So no, to me, there is no such thing as a sacrifice. There are choices and consequences. I did spend a whole chapter on the matter because I really think that it is important and might save you from overpaying to know what is written in the stars: **ALPHAS** are different and won't be able to stand as they were before.

Once you made up your mind, you have to be prepared to unlearn and to relearn most of what you know. If you don't doubt and second-guessing will grind your bones each step of the way.

One of those reference systems is the choice of words you are using. Be careful, words do not simply resonate, but they are powerful in the way you hear and listen to yourself. Using the wrong words will hold you back from your new reality.

Remember the bellybutton, well the wrong set of words will keep it permanently in the center of your field of vision and stain all that will be before your eyes.

This is **AMONGST THE ALPHAS**.

May you find your power in the peace
of knowing what and who you really are.

Dr. BAK NGUYEN

CHAPTER 6
"THE ALPHA GENE?"
BY DR. BAK NGUYEN

By now, I hope you are convinced of the existence of the **ALPHA GENE** within each one of your cells. That's the gene that started our life, that originated our existence.

Talking about the race and the hard survival of life, this is the other 50% talking, standing behind, defensive, waiting to be invaded. Is the picture clear enough? We have both genes encrypted deep in us. We need both genes to be, how we choose to be is up to us.

If you are running a race, the best chance to win, when you are competing against the best is to be better than them. If you are conscious that you are in a race, that your opponent is strong, that you have to tip the edge in your favor, you are playing the game. If you played it better than the other, you will win.

That will make you a winner, not necessarily an Alpha. You see, Alphas do not win, winning is a side effect. And don't get me wrong, they will win, big!

You see, Alphas are freed from their fear. They are focused on their goals, and they will run until they touch that goal and beyond. Even if they will enjoy the game, the rivalry, and the company, all of these are extra and diversion, not the aim.

I am writing those words, but I have to tell you that, I, myself, am not completely over the game, the wins, and the sensations just yet. I still have much to learn and to discover on my **ALPHA JOURNEY**.

I know that I am still attached to the other 50% each time that winning is more important than achieving. It's been a long time since I looked at others as rivals, I see company, that's all.

> "To Alphas, being and doing are important, while winning is a side effect."
> Dr. Bak Nguyen

I love to score, actually, I am addicted to the feeling. I love the impact on the world and how it feels to know that I made a difference.

That should be the ultimate goal, to feel the impact of our actions. In most of my books, I'm always telling you that if you want to build and keep up **Momentum**, you need to feel.

I do, I feel. Do I care if I am the first one at the finished line? Sure, it is fun, the cheering is, the competition is. Those help the feeling good sensation, but how do you explain that I can have the same feeling running on my own, without public, without anyone breathing down my neck?

Oh yes, if you want to be an Alpha, within the first stage, you will be competing, you will be fighting for each inch, each fraction of seconds to be first, and then what? You'll do it all over again?

Maybe a couple of times, just to be better at it and to enjoy the fun, but that's not how you'll build **Momentum**. The best athletes know that too. The real competition, is inside, to outrun those 50% holding you back.

Get good at that game of beating yourself, with kindness and forgiveness, and you will run faster and faster because you are lighter and lighter while getting better and better. Sounds cool?

Trust me, on that, I can tell you that I would never have any world record of any kind if I was focused on trying to score one. The best that would happen is that I spent my entire life trying to find one field to illustrate myself.

Well, I was getting into my forties. A middle-aged man, in the middle of his midlife crisis looking for answers… No, I was looking for motivation. I had many ideas, some great, some less great. Some made it into the blueprints of what put me on the map: **CHANGING THE WORLD FROM A DENTAL CHAIR**!

Is it a race? Sure, one against the odds and against time. I got the idea of running that race the day I stopped looking at my peers and those jealous of my successes as competitors, but as an audience.

If I have helped my patients for nearly 20 years doing something I am great at, but hate; surely I can show my colleagues how it is done and help them find a source of joy and empowerment through their profession.

I am a dentist loved by my patients, by most of them. I am not a self-proclaimed success, they made me into a success at each visit, at each reference, at each return, at each greeting. I gave my best, I was loved and respected.

If you want my secret, I was trying to connect with them, with **kindness**. That was my only way to cope with the fact that I was stuck in a profession not cut for me.

I dropped the regrets and the fear of being judged, not being the best, and all the other side effects that competition will have on a soul.

I was genuine, and I connected. That made me unique, and my patients respond to that, for nearly 20 years. Then, I was about to walk out and to find my destiny when I noticed that I was happy connecting with people, doing something I hate.

My profession suffered from the worse statistics of depression and suicidal rates. How have I beaten all of the odds? That was when I decided to sit down and to look back at my journey to understand.

Then, I started to embrace the stage and the books to share my findings and my personal experience. Doing so, I was the first amongst dentists to care for the well being of my peers, not just their surgical skills. Was I an Alpha yet? Many of my peers were still looking at me as a wannabe, aiming for his hour of fame.

But I was focused on my journey. I never heard the claims nor got down from the hate. Not because I was any stronger or wiser, but because I moved faster than they could react.

They were thinking it, some even expressed it, by the time their opinion reach the public and eventually my ears, I was already 10 miles ahead.

What they based themselves upon to criticize were now a thing of the past. So as my peers were scratching their heads to figure out how to label me, the financial world embraced my views and funded my ideas.

Then, the recognition started to arrive. To face all of those, I needed to be prepared, to be ready. I started writing to get my ideas clear and in order. Well, one chapter after the next, I wrote a book. Then two, then five, and soon enough, I was scoring world record on a monthly basis!

I am talking about world records, I don't even have the time to submit for their officialization and seal of approval. If I wrote 2 books, I would have taken that time, but at the rate of 2 books a month for the last 28 months, I simply couldn't afford the distraction.

Someone from my team will take care of it, eventually. This is my **58th book** within 28 months since I started writing down my thoughts. I have passed the **900,000 words mark**, and I am well on the way to reach the million before 36 months!

Am I an Alpha? Am I a writer? Am I a leader? Well, I do not care how you call me anymore, I just know that I have much fun sharing with you and that I've grown so much so fast that it would be crazy to stop now!

> "The more I write, the more I learn,
> the more I have to share."
> Dr. Bak Nguyen

Did I say that I am having fun? I would never have either started my first chapter if someone were telling me that my goal was to write a book.

I would never have embraced the stage for public speaking if it wasn't because my own company's success depended on the comprehension and support of the public. I am lazy, remember?

Well, on my main race, I am still running the miles to pave the way to an entire industry in crisis. I know that run would end any day soon, and that's okay, I am having fun, much fun. But running that race, I became an Alpha and a unique success story writing words as fast as I speak.

Dr. Bak today is a figure that people are intrigued about, not only the financiers, not only the doctors but the parents, the professors, the men, and the women.

To write the previous words, I had to sit down with my marketing team to understand how my influence has grown. Honestly, I have no clue what I've become and how people see me. I guess I am too busy running and too tired to care.

Running that fast, trust me, I dropped all the burdens and unnecessary weights (values, false beliefs, past glories, and flaws). Running every day, day after day, I mastered the art and lost touch with the boundaries, the gravity.

Each day, at 5 AM, I get to the tracking field, armed with my laptop, my iPhone, and my playlist. I write and share. 500 words soon grew into 1500 words. By now, some of my chapters have more than 3000 words. Not because I want to write more, but that's what got out! And I am too lazy to cut down on my draft.

By the way, for those reading and following my journey, you will know that I rarely use extra words, I do not have the time. I like it straight to the point and to move on to the next issue. As a doctor by trade, I also like proof and a logical explanation of the thought process.

Having to write my first book, **SYMPHONY OF SKILLS**, twice, once in English and then in French within a month (2 weeks each), I also developed a unique writing skill and style. I liked to write speeches and to pace them with the music I listened to while writing them. To me, it is about the words, but most of all, about the sensation.

Well, writing in French, the words couldn't be paced as such. The only way that I found to compensate was to use imagery, metaphors to keep engaging your imagination to force a sensation out of the experience.

Well, I kept that trait as I went back to writing in English. Amongst my 58 books, only 12 are in French. If you must know, that's how I've learnt to write, scoring world record on the way to introduce means and philosophies to save an entire industry!

Now, is that what it means to be an Alpha? Maybe, maybe not. Am I the first, the best? I can tell you that I am actually the only one running this path. The path didn't even exist before my coming.

And for my state of mind? I shared with you that I wasn't looking to score any world record or to write any book, I never thought I had it in me to do either. I just dropped my fears, and my pains, and I started to be. I never stopped since I started, maybe that's the key.

From a loved dentist, one amongst his peers, I rose to serve them with my experience. Today, you are reading my words and debating my thoughts.

You do so because I am not a **wannabe**, well, not anymore. You had the entire process, I never even intended to run this path, but it just happened.

You are reading me and spending time on my thoughts because there is something in this for you. Is it inspiration you seek? Is it knowledge or wisdom you are after? Neither way, you won't be spending time listening and reading the thought of an **arrogant** who is trying to prove that he is better than you.

That too, I passed, a while ago, the day that I grew secure enough to remove myself from the center. Just like I did with my patients the day I grew into a great dentist, putting their interests and concern at the center while I employed and leverage all of myself to deliver. Just like I did with them, you are not reading my thoughts for my benefit, but for yours.

Ever wonder how I could write as much? It is because there is always something else I can help you with! And the more I write, the more I learn, and the more I have to share! What a great recipe to keep you the **relevance**, the **Momentum,** and the **production**!

If I am an Alpha, that's how you came to notice me. But keep in mind that it was a side effect, I never aimed for this, I never thought I had it in me to be this!

> "Mind your goal and its execution,
> the rest will follow accordingly."
> Dr. Bak Nguyen

Well, let me tell you that I never received as much attention and interest. I gained in sex appeal even if I struggle with a weight problem.

My presence on camera is smoother and smoother. Even I, started to like what I see (you have to know that I hate to see myself on video).

And today, most of you met with me through an online video or from a conference you attended. Some I met and greeted in person, but most of you met with me through digital means. Can you believe that I used to suck at those media?

Haven't I told you that back in high school, I was about to fail a French class? And I never truly spoke English fluidly until I embraced the stage a few years back?

I write as I speak. For those of you, loving my style, saying that it is simple and easy to read, that's because I write as I speak.

And even the words, well, I use the words that I know and do the best I can with them!

Can you see there is no big secret nor big revelation! It is only the dropping of my fears and the purge of my pains; the choice to matter, to be useful.

On the way, I learned, I grew secure enough to drop myself from the center of the equation, and the universe revealed itself to me: vast, simple, kind, abundant, and limitless.

When I look at you, I see the universe and its potential. That's why I am kind and humble, confident, and in the mood to share. When I look at how you react to my word, I see myself in your eye, again, I see the universe and its potential. This time, it was my words that painted the portrait.

You should try it, it is a great sensation and an experience of a lifetime.

I was born, just like anyone of you, from an **ALPHA GENE**. For years, I have been trained to ignore that part of me and to repress it down. But something was misplaced, wasn't right. I became a **wannabe** for some time, looking for my footing and my place in life.

Then, I finally found something I am good at. My confidence grew, but I was still **arrogant**. Arrogance became a valued commodity the day people needed it, they then, changed the label from arrogance back to **confidence**.

From confidence, I got much trust and **empowerment to deliver**. With each successful delivery, the trust grew, and so was the confidence. The day I was confident enough to look up, beyond the lies, the conformity, and beyond my bellybutton, that day I discovered true power, I discovered the **Universe and its potential**.

You were looking for a recipe, I gave you better, I gave you my testimony. If you need more proof, you have 57 books to dig into and to retake every step that I took. Do as you feel, do as you must.

You can feel it, can you? That **ALPHA GENE** waking up and flowing your hormones differently? Look in the mirror for the last time, look carefully at what you see. This is society looking back at you.

The next time you need a reflection of yourself, act, do something meaningful, and seek your reflection from the eyes of those you helped. You are an Alpha. And do not stop, your journey is merely beginning! The best is yet to come.

This is **AMONGST THE ALPHAS**.

May you find your power in the peace
of knowing what and who you really are.

Dr. BAK NGUYEN

CHAPTER 7
"THE EVOLUTION OF THE ALPHA?"
BY DR. BAK NGUYEN

We've travelled a long way since the beginning of this journey, the **ALPHA JOURNEY**. I've shared with you a set by step evolution of an Alpha. Most importantly, I've shared with you the Hope that everyone could be an Alpha, it is a matter of choice, yours.

How far are we from your first definition of an Alpha? That Alpha male having most of the women or that Alpha woman with men and women at her feet.

Exchanging with coach Jonas, he shared with me his surprise and enthusiasm by how much we have redefined the term Alpha together. I say together because I explored the angle with you as I was writing, evolving in real-time by your side.

To be honest, if it wasn't for Jonas, I wouldn't have written this book. I would have written another one, covering another subject. Now that I am writing the second to last chapter, I can see how far I went, with you.

The Hope I brought is that we are all Alphas if we choose so. But how about the other Alphas, the strong male, the smart mind, the sexy woman? They received gifts from God, are they more Alphas than any of us?

Well, I started this journey, saying that we, as a species, are on top of the animal kingdom as the dominant species. Based on the old definition of the Alpha, that will mean that we are the strongest, that amongst the wolves, we are the dominant one, that amongst the Apes, we are the strongest.

Well, put our best Alphas, the one that no one will even care to argue about his status. The tallest and the strongest amongst us facing an Alpha Ape, who do you think will come out on top?

Put that same Alpha with the wolves, what are his chance of survival, I am not even addressing the dominance factor yet. As a species, we have managed to be on the top of the animal kingdom thanks to our minds, not our muscles.

We came to dominate the world thanks to our ability to communicate and coordinate our efforts. Without that, we would be far behind in the pyramid of life.

Amongst us, we could distinguish ourselves with those natural attributes of being the tallest, the strongest, but by the end of the day, it is the one that commands the respect of others that will be the leader.

In the past, the lifespan of an individual was a fraction of what it is today. So an Alpha in his prime will be one in his youth, but also one lacking wisdom and experience. For the ladies, that is still the male she wants to copulate with since they both obey the law of natural selection.

Today, this is still something very contemporary in our perception and thinking. That okay, that's natural. The worse thing that we can do is to ignore our biology.

But the matter of this journey was one of much greater importance and scope than to identify those will the best natural genes, gifted from God. **Diversity** has brought so much more to the table, and the criteria of seduction are shifting as we speak.

One hundred years ago, the quarterback and captain America type will have most of the women throwing themselves at him for his DNA potential.

Nowadays, it is the **revenge of the nerds**, the Alpha class is now those smart and somehow socially awkward person trapped in his mind.

Well, since the coming of the information age, those who gained in power are those "**nerds**" changing the world, democratizing technology and information. Well, they got pretty rich, and guess what? Those tools they've invented are empowering more people to gain in power.

"The real use of gunpowder is to make all men tall."
Thomas Carlyle

Since the invention of gunpowder, brutal strength isn't the most important criteria for dominance anymore. In today's military hierarchy, it is often seen that the tallest and strongest is leading a platoon and receiving orders from someone maybe half his size.

Evolution kept us at the forefront of our dominance over the animal kingdom. Before it was about conquering and owning as much as possible, the more, the better.

Well, I won't be telling you anything new, saying that our dominance on this planet is about to end if we are still taking without **giving back**!

Now that we have discovered all the lands, have "conquered" most of the species, we are more vulnerable than ever because the next menace is one that we do not see.

Our next war isn't one with an enemy with a face, but one we cannot see. A mutation of the bacteria flora could wipe us off the surface of the planet. Our own dominance has pushed us to the blink of destruction since we are taking more from mother Earth than she could regenerate herself.

Even those battles that we won, killing those beast-eating men, well, we are unbalancing the cycle of life with effects that will ripple for generations after we are gone.

All of those, it is not the muscles that will present the needed leverage to survive and to get to the next level.

It is not intelligence solely either. We've been pretty smart for the last couple of centuries, and look where it brought us. No, being an Alpha today has changed much with the centuries of civilization and evolution.

I would say that today, to be an Alpha, one needs the heart to care for things bigger than him or herself. But that alone is not enough since we live in a **self-empowerment era** in which, to be well and happy, now and today, is everyone's right and goal.

I am not criticizing that, but not at all. On the contrary, I really think that it took so much evolution and philosophy for us to be able to build upon the shoulders of our ancestors to arrive at this point.

> "We are the dominant species because we have learnt to network over time and space."
> Dr. Bak Nguyen

That's how we are building from one generation to the next. The industrialization era brought us to be able to mass-produce and democratized commodities and tools to leverage our life upon. It has allowed the age of self-empowerment.

Well, the information age is just that, to democratize the available knowledge and how to put it to good use. There was a time where knowledge is power. Today, a quick search on Google and most knowledge is available to everyone, to anyone.

With the spending of the internet network and the improvement of technology, even the speed of delivery is not as crucial as an issue anymore. So what will define the Alpha of tomorrow?

Vision and the will to do good. More than smart, the Alpha will have to be wise and to counterbalance his or her actions over the whole system. **Wise** because it isn't enough to be smart and to win anymore, knowing that there is a cost to that win.

The Alphas of tomorrow are ones that will build and improve knowing what he or she is reporting as a cost to the next generations.

No one is perfect, as no system is perfect. The only thing we can do is to do the best with what we have in hand today, but now, we must also understand and weigh its consequences over time.

This isn't philosophy and positive thinking, if we do not shift our vision and leadership as we speak, well, our whole species will be wiped out from this planet, and an alternative life form will take over where we left.

Look at the age of the universe. Let's make it easier, just look at the age of our planet, it is approximated at 4.543 billion years. Our existence on this planet is approximated at 200,000 years, which represents 0.0044% of the existence of the Earth. Are you still thinking that we are a dominant and important species?

This is just if we look in time, do not forget the space factor? Are we the only dominant and intelligent life form in the universe? We are a small step in a much bigger whole. Yet, how about the significance of a person in this scope?

Let say that our Alpha is changing the world and make it a better place. His or her total lifespan, let's give him or her 80 on today's standard. That's 0.04% compared to the existence of our kind (80 years over 200 000).

And that's considering that that individual was the only one of importance. Usually, we should divide it again by the total number of individuals alive for that same period. Today, we are nearly 6 billion people, so that will be 0.04% divided by 6 billion people!

> "Do you realize how many zeros after the coma that makes us?"
> Dr. Bak Nguyen

So how important is the Alpha? The point here is not to see how little our bellybutton really is, but how big is the obstruction it censors us from reality, and you will understand the real meaning of Alpha.

We've been a long way since the beginning. We did so because we've evolved and adapted from stage to stage, changing our leverage and adapting to the new and bigger challenges.

This quest of being an Alpha is a personal one, but also one that could make the difference between evolution or extinction. Earth, nature, the universe will be there long after we cease to exist. How long will be our existence and how relevant it will be, is for us to decide.

Our forefathers and foremothers have built much since we first appear on this planet. Be grateful and thank them for their vision, for their successes, for their failures from which we are learning. Being an Alpha does not mean to be the best amongst us anymore, but **being one with the universe**.

If today we have the chance to think as a species, to compare how little we are in comparison cease the planet we received, for the next 80 years, it is because we've built on the shoulders of those who preceded us.

What was good enough yesterday is today a new standard. What is standard today, well, will be obsolete by tomorrow. This is the game of evolution.

> "Everything changes and evolves,
> so will the Alphas, to keep their relevancy."
> Dr. Bak Nguyen

That how today, the "nerds" got their revenge. That class of people bullied and left behind a century ago are today the dominant class of the modern world.

They will change society and reshape the world from their thoughts and work. Today, intelligence and wisdom are key to being an Alpha, a leader, someone with the power to make a difference. Tomorrow, what will be the new criteria?

Well, it will still start with those ready to leave the past behind and willing to embrace the unknown with hope. Leaving the past means purging the fear, the old ways, the old certainties.

Embracing the new means to be secure enough to look beyond oneself and to be able to absorb the next layer of information. I said next because it wasn't new. The information was always there, but only now are we capable of absorbing it.

And about the **ALPHA GENE** versus the **God-given ALPHANESS**? Well, let face it, the **ALPHA GENE** is our ultimate legacy from life itself. This is the core. For those who received a little more from the trade, well, they receive both a gift and a handicap.

How so? Being pretty, smart, strong, or tall is surely a big plus. But it is a starting point, not the final destination. Those who will understand that and leverage upon their God-given gift to push themselves furthermore on the evolution scale, would have succeeded more than the average amongst us. That's the gift.

The trap is to sit on that advantage. It won't be too long before most of the God-given attributes won't be enough to put them ahead of the curve.

As the average will be catching up, those sitting on their God-given talents won't have the right mindset to adapt and to improve.

Well, they will be swallowed by the average and may end up last, way behind… because they never adapted.

> "This game is the game of evolution,
> you can win if you do not evolve.
> Well, motivation is a pretty strong leverage."
> Dr. Bak Nguyen

This is **AMONGST THE ALPHAS**.

May you find sure power in the peace
of knowing what and who you really are

Dr. BAK NGUYEN

CHAPTER 8
"THE ALPHAS' DAILY?"
BY DR. BAK NGUYEN

Already we are at the last chapter of the **ALPHA JOURNEY**. What started as a subject that I considered for being a label allowed me the opportunity to share with all of you the Hope of a better tomorrow within each of us.

But there is still so much more to say about the Alpha! Not to leave you on your appetite, we spent the last two chapters proving that everyone can become an Alpha, from my own personal journey and then, the necessity of evolving as Alphas, in the grand scheme of our species.

I hope that you picked up on the vibe and the opportunity, but also on the urgency of the situation to rise to your rightful place in the **Universe**.

Much has changed in your conception of this mystic word, **ALPHA**. Let take it back a step and go back at the Alpha in everyday life. After all, we have to evolve from where we stand, the current limitations and horizon.

What is the main advantage of being an Alpha?

Well, if this isn't clear enough, let me clarify it once more. An Alpha is one that freed him or herself from the fear, in other words, the past.

Somehow, that Alpha sees the future as it should be, and will build the bridge between that projected future and the present where he or she is standing.

That's the definition, that's the purpose of an Alpha. Doing so the Alpha is drafting the future or will die trying. Since we have developed the ability to network through time and space, another Alpha will take over where this one left, and eventually, a bridge will be built.

> "Alphas will always win the war, if not today, well, they will in a few generations."
> Dr. Bak Nguyen

I used the word war to appeal to your imagination and the themes we love. But don't mistake the word, Alphas build more than they destroy, that the whole purpose of being an Alpha in the first place, is to build the future.

Are there any immediate advantages of being an Alpha? More than having the women and the men? Just kidding… Before an Alpha could benefit from any social leverage, he or she will be heavily tested by those he or she grew up with.

Once he or she has accepted his true calling, he will walk alone for a while. That's how his or her character will start forging, stronger, and more resilient. Alphas are Alphas because they do not need the empowerment of the crowd to keep moving forward.

If you consider motivation a must, this is one of the key advantages of the Alphas, they **self-motivate**. Some Alphas will start from the frustration and the anger that most people discredited them. That frustration will fuel their advancement for a little while, but won't be enough to fulfil the whole journey.

Consider that frustration as a boost to start, until they find the footing and the conviction within.

> "For an Alpha, the answer is often from within…"
> Dr. Bak Nguyen

And then, he or she will have to apply it to the external world. And the only way to find that motivation within was to open and to look up. It is only as one looks at the Universe and feels something real inside that the **ALPHA GENE** will activate.

This is how one will surpass the stage of wannabe and arrogant. If one keeps looking at his or her belly button, he or she might have started the journey, on the beginner slope but never actually got on top of the mountain to ski. Trust me, the view, the feeling is from another level, completely.

About the other advantages, I will say that they are more side effects than advantages. But once **self-motivated**, the Alpha will start achieving results above average. As he or she keeps pushing, the results will define new possibilities and new standards.

From that point, followers will start gathering. Both men and women will be intrigued by how that Alpha has been able to do the impossible.

Since nothing of worth can be achieved alone, the Alpha will now have to learn to communicate and to work with a team, teaching, training, coaching, and motivating others.

I said that it is more a side effect than an advantage because most Alphas will find themselves slowed down by the rise in interest and popularity. Frustrations and distractions now pave the **ALPHA JOURNEY**.

> "Being an Alpha is a state of mind. It has to be leveraged and put into motion to last."
> Dr. Bak Nguyen

That's another reality, Alphaness is not a permanent status nor condition, it is a choice that has to be renewed on a daily basis. Eventually, the choice is made out with the force of habit, but still, every Alpha will have to renew their choice and commitment from time to time.

> "Being an Alpha is being a champion."
> Dr. Bak Nguyen

No one can remain a champion for life. But one can keep the flame alive and keep pushing with the same mindset. **Self-motivation**, that's the main advantage of being an Alpha.

In what kind of situations an Alpha shouldn't reveal him or herself?

Well, that's a tricky question. An Alpha is a state of mind, one that has a higher spirit. Even a blind person will see the Alpha arriving from miles away.

Now, since evolution, everyone can choose to grow into an Alpha. Not necessarily taller or smarter, but there is something more about those people that gloom in the dark, even in the middle of the day. That flame can hardly be hidden.

The rebellious spirit that you can see in someone's eyes, that's the **ALPHA GENE** walking up. That's the refusal to give up, that's the **ALPHA GENE** talking. That's bad boy spirit, that's **God-given attitude** shadowing the Alpha.

We all have it in us. Some will embrace it as a child. Some will only discover it much later in life. Some will always fear its presence, spending their entire life burying it. It is a choice, nothing more.

So, of course, there are many situations where to be the underdog or to be invisible is better than to be presented as the champion. Well, for those in disguise, most of these weren't Alphas at the beginning, they became Alpha on the way.

Some are masters of disguise and will succeed to fool most of us, but even then, there were traces of strength to be noticed, we simply weren't smart and quick enough to pick up on them.

In other words, from a strategic standpoint, rarely it is an advantage to be presented as Alpha, it is more a liability. But since **Alphaness** is not simply a coat we pick up and remove at will, most Alphas will have to learn to deal with it.

The first time one will try on the coat, it will be exhilarating and mind-blowing. Then, he or she will face the rejection and the hate of mostly everyone he or she knows. If he survives that, he will be ready for more, more rejections, more challenges, more traps.

As the old saying says, it never gets easier, we just grow stronger. That's the fate of the Alpha.

What are the risks of being an Alpha?

That one should be obvious by now: to be rejected and isolated, and then, to bear the weight of the world on our shoulders. But most Alphas have to escape that fatality.

Remember that I told you that not all Alphas are leaders? Why do you think that is? Mr. Nice Guy is the one everyone will go to complain about. If things are going well, okay, but as soon as things are going south, Mr. Nice Guy will be held responsible for the fate of the world...

Well, don't forget that if Mr. Nice Guy is an Alpha, he is much smarter and wiser than you are. Also, if he is an Alpha, he knows his strength and will deliver on them, but once that's done, he will usually find a way to fade from the public eye... not to be bothered bearing the weight of the world, even when he has the skills to leverage the next round.

Not all Alphas are as smart or as wise, but History will teach all of them, talking about power.

> "Power isn't something you hold too tight close to your chest since it might kill you."
> Dr. Bak Nguyen

Some will live to tell the tale, others, well, will be the tale to be told. So if you ask me was is the danger of being an Alpha, I think that the real danger is to think that the state is permanent and will last forever.

Be wise enough to learn from legends and History, since the story is always the same one, over and over again, with different disguises and decors.

Don't let the Alphaness go to your head! Keep both your heart and mind open and the answer will come to you naturally: when to be and when to leave.

How should an Alpha surround him or herself?

The first thing to understand and to accept as an Alpha is to be ready to walk alone. He or she have to be open and ready to share, but the Alpha will always be betting on him or herself first.

Eventually, the fight will be so much bigger than him or herself that he or she will need to network and combine to achieve a victory. The first stage is often to connect with a more experienced soul, a mentor.

> "To mentor an Alpha, one has to be an Alpha himself."
> Dr. Bak Nguyen

For the mentor, mentoring a younger Alpha is the chance to do it again, maybe better and bigger. To the young protege, learning from a mentor will save him much time and mistakes on a way full of challenges and insecurities. Both have something unique and of great worth to gain out of the trade.

Other than the mentor, the journey of an Alpha will eventually lead him or her to meet with allies. Some times Alphas, some times not. Those people will be joining the quest of a moment, sharing a common goal. They will leave by the completion of that common goal.

Rivals are Alphas that are running the same race. They might not be playing for the same team, but they want the exact same goal. They too, have an important role in the quest, since they will be putting peer pressure over the Alpha.

We know that an Alpha self-motivate. Well, with the presence of a mentor, the motivation is amplified by much. With the presence of a rival, time now becomes a crucial element in the equation. The journey just became a race. And nothing is a better motivation booster than a lack of time!

Enjoy the company while it lasts. Company, mentor, competition, connect with the vibe, and be your best, the best you did not know you had in you until that point. This is what the surrounding of an Alpha will bring out of him or her.

> "The worse that could happen to an Alpha is not to be alone, but to be surrounded by Betas with love."
> Dr. Bak Nguyen

Between an average company and no company, an Alpha is better off on his own. This does not mean that he is snob, but playing amongst Alphas will keep his motivation up. To help and to empower those willing to evolve, the motivation is there.

Those who are toxic are the ones thinking that they found and have all the answers that they need. Until that point, this is still okay, but those people have a heavy tendency not to move forward and to condemn anyone who would! Fighting that fight is a pure loss of time... and worse, of moral.

How can an Alpha inspire instead of imposing? Well, this one is obvious. Remember the nature of the Alpha was to dump his **FEAR** and to grow secure enough to look up.

Only when he or she is finally looking up that the power and potential of the universe will be within reach. That power is what makes the Alpha so powerful... eventually.

> "Now, what is authority? Who is looking to impose? Basically those with insecurity."
> **Dr. Bak Nguyen**

So no, an Alpha will never sacrifice his connection with the universe and the unlimited power in exchange for authority. Not all Alphas are leaders... and unfortunately, now you see it too, not all leaders are Alphas.

That should wrap it up about the authority figure. Now, about inspiring, well, remember the chapter on mentors, why an Alpha will mentor a younger one? And the passage of how why the Alpha are sharing? It is because those are means for them to access a higher level of energy.

Training the next generation and empowering the future potential will either gave them a second chance to do more with less or to reignite their own flame to the next level. To share and to inspire are not burdens to those who've walked it. Trust me, that talk isn't cheap!

So the question was how… I gave you the why. Now, how is an Alpha empowering and inspiring the crowd and those looking up at him or her?

Well, by sharing his journey, his failures, and how he dealt with them. If he is there, talking, that meant that he made it out alive, so what did he learn? And of course, he will be back to transform that failure into his next stepping stone.

To an Alpha, everything is a stepping stone. Some will be named different as a cornerstone, but by the end of the day, those are all stone he stepped on to keep moving. Even if he built a bridge to the future, once the bridge is complete, he will move on, that's his destiny, his DNA.

All of those walking that bridge might or might not know who built it at first. Those who know will eventually show gratitude. That's the beginning of the enlightenment, to recognize the past achievements and to show **gratitude**.

> "Gratitude and fear don't mix well. The more grateful you are, the less fearful you'll grow."
> Dr. Bak Nguyen

Gratitude is often the first step to awareness, one that might open the doors to a fearless life. In other words, gratitude is the beginning of the **ALPHA JOURNEY**. I can stretch enough the importance of gratitude.

> "Gratitude is the only past with a future."
> Dr. Bak Nguyen

I love that quote. The more I write it, the more I stand by each of those words. Now, we understand what future we are talking about since the Alphas draft the Future from the strength of their mind and their imagination.

How powerful is that, to create the future with our mind and heart? Is it creativity or the expression of the Universe? Who cares? Really! Create once, and you will feel the power and the feeling good vibe coming with it.

And in that feeling good vibe, it becomes easier to open up to the universe and to see more, to receive more, to do more. **More**, that's what and how the Universe is offering.

And who has access to the universe, all of us, but some don't look up and miss on the better part of life. Well, those looking up and ascending with their connection to the universe, those are the ones we call Alphas.

"Don't look for approval, look to overwhelm. And then, do not care and keep doing it."
Dr. Bak Nguyen

This is **AMONGST THE ALPHAS**.

May you find your power in the peace
of knowing what and who you really are

Dr. BAK NGUYEN

PART II
BY GUEST AUTHORS

CHAPTER 9
"ALPHAS, I KNOW, I LOVE"
BY DR. MARIA KUNSTADTER

I am delighted to be included as a guest author for this book. As I revisit my perspectives on being an Alpha and its ramifications, being "included" is often lacking in the life of an Alpha.

I appreciate Dr. Bak for putting a finger on the pulse of **Alpha psychology**, from the genetic makeup in all of us to the societal need to pressure everyone into *conformity*. I also relish the opportunity to walk **"Amongst the Alphas"** and the affirmations of being identified as part of that group.

As much as the United States claims rights to individual freedoms, most humans exercise that freedom by aligning with a group. Psychology has established our basic needs for social identity, that identity is a person's sense of who they are based on their group membership.

Henri Tajfel first proposed this in 1979 and he proposed that groups such as family, social class, football teams, and political parties which people *"belonged to"* were an essential part of a person's self-esteem and provided a sense of belonging to the social world.

> "Society has set up conformity as a comfort zone."
> Dr. Maria Kunstadter

This conformity to a group's dogma provides security. Religion isn't the only group that has dogma but is also steeped in dogmatic rituals and traditions. *"Tradition"* is sung loudly and passionately by Tevye, the Papa in Fiddler on the Roof.

Those *"traditions"* provided Papa and members of other religions around the world a feeling of belonging to a group identity. Repeated mantras that others are also engaged in helps block the fear of the unknown. Conformity, routine, rituals all provide stability and security.

As an Alpha, that group identity is illusive. One of the ways it starts, very early in life, is when a child is identified by classmates as the **teacher's pet**. Singled out to be a helper due to characteristics the teacher subconsciously identified as more capable, mature, brighter or advanced, the teacher's attention is obvious to other students and the "**pet**" becomes a target of disdain from everyone else.

I was that student — no one likes the **teacher's pet** because it makes the other students feel *"less"* special.

> "Most people, even children,
> are comfortable set in the average."
> **Dr. Maria Kunstadter**

An Alpha make those people feel badly. That designation of *"special"* doesn't have an external stigma, but as an Alpha, it sometimes feels like there is an "A" emblazoned somewhere on my person like that in the Scarlett Letter, that others see.

The definition of a *stigma* is a *"mark of disgrace* that sets a person apart from others. Beliefs toward this group create prejudice which leads to negative actions and discrimination". Though being an Alpha is not a disgrace, it still sets one apart from others and that distinction leads to negative actions of avoidance, lack of understanding, and isolation.

> "The Alpha road is not always a choice, but the realization that you don't fit in anywhere else, so traveling life alone is the only option."
> Dr. Maria Kunstadter

Finding another Alpha or two other Alphas throughout your life helps, but we Alphas aren't good at relationships because of our lifelong isolation. As Jerry Seinfeld said, "Sometimes the road less traveled is less traveled for a reason."

Being a non-conformist is a blessing and a curse. Choosing that different path might be lonely, but to explore the world with unique eyes and experiences is a thrill only those that express their **Alpha nature** get to have. Great things never came from comfort zones.

> "Only those who risk going too far find out how far one can go."
> TS Elliot

As a woman, my *Alpha vision* has been stifled by sexism, and so I appreciate the fact that I am part of an Alpha group — not just a group of Alpha males as we standardly hear about. I do love the quote from Robert Kennedy, even if it addresses "men".

> "Some men see things as they are and ask, why?
> I dream things that never were and ask, why not?"
> Robert Kennedy

That is what defines me. We are all given the vision to see beyond the average daily tasks. Alphas act on that vision. It has taken me a lifetime to sit back and feel good about being unique, different, isolated from the norm, but I can now say I wouldn't have wanted to be any other way. I feel I have a big responsibility to use my skills for the betterment of society.

> "The *why not* vision opens up limitless possibilities
> I feel compelled to explore."
> Dr. Maria Kunstadter

I dedicate this chapter to my children who are walking this walk and coming to terms with their *uniqueness* as a benefit to themselves and the world around them. I have walked this walk for more than six decades, unaffiliated with group identity and always feeling it was because there was something *wrong* with me.

There is something so *right* in my children and all the Alphas out there, so don't shrink from your vision because others can't handle being in your orb! We have all dealt with the *"popular"* crowd as the in-group and the challenge is to overcome not being accepted into that group.

The *"strength"* of the in-group always rallies around pointing out negative aspects of an outsider in order to enhance their self-image.

> "The *strength of an Alpha* is the wonderful fact that you are not compelled to bend towards acceptance and limit your potential."
> **Dr. Maria Kunstadter**

The genetic component plays out so strongly in the women in my family. It is important for my children to know that they come from a long lineage that expressed their **Alpha nature**.

Great grandmothers on both sides of my family left their home countries and sailed across the ocean to a new home where they knew no one, didn't speak the language. They established families and became part of the community around them. At 22 years old, one great-grandmother made that journey alone. Another great-grandmother married and then came over as a new wife to a new land.

Strength to be unique and independent didn't begin with them, but they exemplified Alpha characteristics long ago. My grandmother married outside her religion, which was unheard of in her era and she and my grandpa were always outsiders, for being in a mixed marriage and both being exceptionally bright! The strength to exercise non-conformity is as strong in our lineage as it is in all of us. One must embrace it.

> "To accept your own potential without arrogance or pride is a big part of greatness."
> Dr. Maria Kunstadter

As Dr. Bak said, "Sit on your God-given talent or raise the average". That choice is a call on which to respond. An Alpha is. The difference making an Alpha is the courage to resist conformity and society's need to squelch achievement and to accept the *uniqueness* as a tool to accomplish many things.

> "The only thing standing between me and greatness is me".
> Woody Allen

Now that I have *actualized* myself, the tasks that lie ahead are daunting. Again, quoting Dr. Bak, he says to be "grateful and graceful". Pride or self-adulation will limit success. To move forward with other Alphas makes the opportunities open-up even more and successful accomplishments become more of a reality.

The privilege is not taken for granted but has empowered unleashed potential. My name is Dr. Maria Kunstadter and I am an Alpha. With gratitude.

This is **AMONGST THE ALPHAS**.

May you find your power in the peace
of knowing what and who you really are.

Dr. BAK NGUYEN

CHAPTER 10
"PROUD TO BE AN ALPHA"
BY DR. PAUL OUELLETTE

My name is Dr. Paul Ouellette. I have been an Orthodontist now for 50 years! If I could practice another 50 years you would still see me working with my two sons and Alpha colleagues for another half-century. We are a truly blessed profession!

What we do is fun, usually appreciated and we provide first-class care, beautiful smiles, and comfort for our patients. We are Smile Stylists who sell beauty and self-confidence. What is more fun than that? This is *why* I stay active in my profession.

During the 2020 Covid 19 Pandemic we were all locked down from March of 2020 for 3 or more months. I was furloughed by the corporate practice I was working for at the time and not offered a contract to return. I was one of the top four earners in my offices and management replaced all of us with recently graduated orthodontic residents from Georgia School of Orthodontics.

Prior to taking the job offer with the corporate DSO three years before, I was an Associate Professor of Orthodontics at **GSO** - Georgia School of Orthodontics. Two of my orthodontic faculties and myself were the first professors recruited to open the largest orthodontic program in the world in a northern suburb of Atlanta.

I was the program's first clinical director. The first 20 residents graduated in August of 2020, the year of the great Pandemic. Most were able to get jobs in their hometowns or in the metro Atlanta suburbs. I believe our first graduating class all found positions. I was so proud of my residents even though three of them replaced me in my 3 offices.

> "One door slammed shut in my face, but two or more doors opened with a more promising future."
> Dr. Paul Ouellette

One of the doors opened when I met my brother from another mother Dr. Bak Nguyen founder of the Alphas. He called me out of the blue. He was doing a series of interviews with other dentists in the USA, Canada, South America, and Europe.

I am proud to be his first or second member of the Alphas. I was either Bak's first Alpha or our colleague Dr. Eric LACOSTE, Periodontist and MBA, was number two. It doesn't matter as we are all equal and shared our experiences and ideas with the group.

Dr. Lacoste, MBA, is a community leader, twice DUNAMIS laureate, HOMAGE from the Quebec Dentists Order, and winner of the TELUS Social Implication Award. It does not really matter as all our recruits are leaders in their communities and recognized for many accomplishments during their careers in Dentistry.

> "Alphas are the shakers and movers of our industry."
> Dr. Paul Ouellette

Together we are discussing the future of Dentistry post-pandemic. Collectively the Alphas shared ideas during a long summer and fall in Zoom conferences. The goal was to share old and new ideas to give our profession hope for the future.

Let me share a little about the characteristics of the Alphas. My Alpha brothers and sisters are **empathic** primarily focusing on others before themselves. My Alpha colleagues encourage strategic thinking, are innovators, and ethical professionals. We are civic-minded and charitable.

We are Key Opinion Leaders in our local and international professional communities. Dr. Bak is internationally recognized on Linkedin and other social media platforms. He was honored as one of the 100 Top Dentists in the World in 2021. Dr. Bak unified leaders in our profession, bankers, Ted Talk celebrities, and other professionals that could share ideas for how to come out the other side of the Global Pandemic.

One of the projects that evolved from our summer discussions was related to the fear of aerosols in bricks and mortar medical or dental buildings was a mobile cargo trailer dental clinic project.

We planned to find a way to treat the trailer's inside air to hospital-grade. Using HEPA and ultraviolet light air scrubbers was our plan. I initially purchased a Mercedes Extended Wheelbase Travel Coach to convert into an Ortho "Scan Van".

When laying out places for a dental chair or chairs, a digital panoramic machine, and sterilization center there was not enough room for everything needed to deliver mobile orthodontic aligner services. My initial thought was to add a small utility pull behind the trailer to power the Sprinter. We would use propane gas generators placed on the extended tongue of the small cargo trailer.

In addition, the water and sewer services would be placed in the trailer to avoid foul-smelling system in the Sprinter. The cargo trailer would be lower than the elevated Sprinter to easily establish a fall for drainage.

Several Alphas helped me with the project especially Dr. Maria Kunstadter, Dentist, and co-founder of THETELEDENTISTS.COM (the biggest teledentistry provider in the USA). In addition, Dr. Julio Reynafarje, Dean of the Peruvian Dental Association postgraduate School of continued Education, and Dr. Jeremy Krell, Dentist, MBA, and serial entrepreneur, the real definition of an OVERACHIEVER.

Dr. Paul Dominique, a pediatric dentist who joined the profession at 27 years old played a key role as an advisor. From public dental health, he moved on to build a network of clinics and sold them to a Dental Service Organization. Now, at 50, he is half retired and is investing in different dental tech companies, including teledentistry. Dr. Dominique is one of the principal investors in THETELEDENTISTS.COM.

Maria and Paul will be helping with the practice management, billing, and insurance filing for the project. My goal will be initially to support the larger referrers of Specialty procedures that are not offered in their practices such as Pediatric and Orthodontic services. If a General Practioner refers out his or her pedodontic and orthodontic procedures, the mobile trailers will have two dental chairs, a digital panorex, and a sterilization center.

The mobile dental trailers are 16 feet long by 8 feet wide to fit into a standard-sized car parking place. One mobile cargo trailer will have 2 dental chairs, a digital panoramic machine, and a sterilization center.

We will use modified computer gaming chairs instead of conventional "expensive" dental chairs that often give a young patient anxiety or fear of getting into the threatening dental chair. The gaming chair tops will be attached to 4" diameter boat pedestals with a motorized lifting system. The cost of the modified chairs is $300 or less for each, compared to several thousand-dollar dental chairs. Gaming chairs have waterproof coverings that are bright and exciting for the young patient compared to a sometimes scary dental chair.

The inside of the trailers will be themed by the IDSkids.com in Canada as described on their website. "Imagination Design Studios (formerly Imagination Dental Solutions) creates custom-themed environments that make appointments easy and stress-free for your young patients and their parents.

With over 450 themed dental offices, hospitals, optometry clinics, and more, **IDS** is the only theming company with over a decade of specialized experience in serving dental and medical professions. When you combine the exceptional service provided by you and your team, and blend that together with an unforgettable environment, you create the most memorable patient experience."

In the past 50 years of practicing specialty dentistry, our family has opened several offices that were, in most cases, themed. We want our patients to have an "experience" they will always remember and tell their friends about. I highly recommend the IDSkids creative designs to create exciting interiors and exteriors, especially for the apprehensive patients.

Bricks and mortar dental offices of the future do not have to have large waiting rooms. During the Covid lockdown my son Dr. Jason Ouellette, Orthodontist, perfected the *"parking lot"* consultation. When patients arrive, they text the office to let us know they are here for their scheduled appointment. We then text them when it's their turn to come into the reception area for fever screening and to sign covid release forms. After the patients go to the clinic for their orthodontic adjustment or pediatric appointment, they are dismissed and return to their car.

Dr. Jason would often accompany his patients to their parent's car. He would then have an informal consultation with the attending parent. If Dr. Jason was not available, one of his

Team Members would do the post-appointment consultations. His patients and parents just waited in their automobiles.

Why do we have to build a large waiting room in future dental or medical offices? The future dental medical office park may be designed more like an RV-Recreational Vehicle park with a covered outdoor Pavilion for patients and accompanying guardians to wait in a *social distancing* configuration. The parking lot would be designed with covered walkways for inclement weather.

I envision a hub and spoke design with mobile medical dental trailer pads for two or more attached *trailer clinics*. The medical professional could set a schedule to move from location to location each week of the day.

> "Bricks and Mortar clinic
> may one day become obsolete."
> **Dr. Paul Ouellette**

I want to thank my Alpha colleagues for sharing their ideas and constructive comments that will help us develop a new mobile concept for the dental offices of the future. My name is Dr. Paul Ouellette and I am an Alpha.

This is **AMONGST THE ALPHAS**.

May you find your power in the peace
of knowing what and who you really are.

Dr. BAK NGUYEN

CHAPTER 11
"SOLUTION SEEKERS"
BY DR. JEREMY KRELL

Being an Alpha, to me, is about navigating the tricky traps that whatever life throws at you. But being an Alpha is more than being a survivor, it is about finding the solution and surfing the challenges. Alphas do so while welcoming the collaboration with other Alphas.

Remember when you first got your driver's license? Remember the first ride you took alone? The first time you got lost alone? I have spent most of my time in start-ups, which means working through uncertain times and ambiguity, so the real-world cases and solutions I present below, are the tale of one Alpha.

I am a non-traditional dentist, who found his way into the art of business while pursuing clinical dentistry. I didn't get there on my own by any means. I had several mentors, doctors, and people who believed in me even when I failed and I doubted myself.

I connected with a mentor who led a department in my dental school. He had a background in plastics engineering and was a true innovator. As I was looking to find my ways back at school between dentistry and entrepreneurship, he guided me. A true Alpha. Not only did he support me in this way, but he spoke to me, in a way another Alpha would, and told me it was okay to pursue other interests.

He had it all: a private practice, an academic career, a war chest of inventions. His background inspired me to pursue my dream to create products and services and reach the level of an Alpha.

The chicken or the egg first? I call it the *"chegg".*

> *"Dreams are nothing if not for the triumph over challenges along the way - this is a common ambition among alphas."*
> **Dr. Jeremy Krell**

An Alpha is a solution seeker, an eternal solution seeker. I have dubbed some common vicious cycles, aka chicken or the egg situations, in entrepreneurship as *"cheggs."*

Cheggs occur when you have something of value on the line, like an idea or startup, and you perceive your choices as *lose-lose*. In these issues, I wish I had an Alpha relationship, as we are quite collaborative, to advise me along the way.

Instead, I learnt the hard way, making my mistake on the field. They aren't unique challenges, but they do present different perspectives. So, as an Alpha, here are my thoughts on how to navigate these tricky little traps.

The first of these common challenges is **commitment**. I've spent energy, time, money, and dedication to become a doctor. I love helping people, but I found out that I can also help people being an entrepreneur. As I learnt from my mentor, an

Alpha does not necessarily have to choose one over the other. If I am smart enough to think outside of the box, I can do them both successfully, I can have it all!

> "To think outside of the box is a key trait of Alphas."
> Dr. Jeremy Krell

There is always a way and even a better way! Seek for the solution! For as long as you are committed, you will prevail. This is part of being an Alpha.

A second chegg is now or later? And later, well, we have a word for it, it is called procrastination. Smart people, the smarter they are, the more excuses they will come up with to whether or not to justify the delay of actions and decisions.

Here is how I defeat procrastination every time it surfaces: consider the fact that your idea may not have a shelf life of "forever" as few things do. If we think we can help a situation (problem), we have the duty to pursue that goal, as each additional procedure rendered with a more ideal product or service could change the outcome.

Someone else might pursue your idea very similarly, rendering your pursuit obsolete, or at least, very different chasing an incumbent. Besides competition, you need to think about the team. This means assembling people or entities (that you like) whose backgrounds match with what you're trying to do.

The market opportunity is also important, market dynamics change, some are more volatile than others, but this can open and shut opportunities.

Lastly, the product will move forward by means of manpower to, at the very least, validate the idea. My best advice here is that if the above align, you should roll the dice and take a chance. No regret, do and learn.

Alphas are leaders and stand on their own. Not necessarily. If we replace the word Alpha with a trending one, entrepreneur, all entrepreneurs will tell you that to realize an idea, one needs finances and money. So no, no Alpha, no entrepreneur can make it on his or her own.

When it comes to finance my ideas, here is a chegg around having enough revenue to fundraise. You need more customers, but in order to get them, you need more money.

First, back up, and look to exhaust all free and very cheap ways to get customers or revenue. There is a lot of free press, podcast/webinar features (during Covid-19, a startup in my portfolio grew 40% this way), influencers, email campaigns, and more that fit the ticket.

Second, there are proxies for revenue, like customers and engagement. It isn't just about dollar flow. Showing that you have built something that people like to use is valuable, even without a clear revenue stream or path to profitability developed yet.

> "Being able to draw attention and interest in something, even when objective measures aren't clear, is something I learnt as an Alpha."
> Dr. Jeremy Krell

As I said before, an Alpha is a **solution seeker**. An Alpha needs to be confident enough to stand on his or her own, but also, humble enough to accept help when needed.

Now, an Alpha does not wait for help to come, in the meantime, the Alpha will work an angle to move towards the solution. And often, in my career, that was where I grew and learnt much. At the end of the day, if you **like what you are doing**, you will never work a day in your life.

> "Improvement is always necessary, but not always welcomed."
> Dr. Jeremy Krell

As an Alpha, I strongly advise you to always keep an open mind to seek a better way, even if things are working. The thought process should always go back and forth between why and why not. Even if the solution in hand is working.

Everything can be improved, remember that! As an Alpha, you will be pushing multiple fronts forward. Keep delivering the present solution while being open for more, for better!

As an entrepreneur, an Alpha, you are considering entering a world of commercializing new innovations. Just like everything that you've done until now, there will be a first. Like anything else, seek help, learn, question, and be open to learn and to relearn.

> "True innovation strategy involves a thorough investigation and validation process."
> Dr. Jeremy Krell

Asking for help and trusting the party helping you is key to success and to rise as an Alpha. As an Alpha who has worked on the business side of the industry, I can attest to the frequency of *cheggs* that occur throughout the process as well as the need for a relatable pathway to foster the innovation process, specifically that of medical professionals.

These can be confusing and frustrating pitfalls. It takes real assertiveness and awareness to know that you have fallen into the trap. Alphas are frequently coming up with new frameworks.

Doctors take signs and symptoms into account, followed by testing, they employ deductive reasoning to hone in on a diagnosis. A very similar process applies in business when entrepreneurs see processes start to spin or go sideways and sometimes they may need outside help to break the cycle.

Sometimes, we think we can do everything well, but as we try new things, we are bound to find obstacles we have never encountered before. Just as with medical training, where you are educated by another medical professional who has done those procedures before, you need to be able to do the same in business.

An alpha is not a know-it-all nor a one-man show. An Alpha is a solution seeker. An Alpha is a team player when it is required. But an Alpha will not mind walking alone if this is where the solution lays.

In the medical field, some Alpha will bear the title of doctor. In the business world, they are innovators and entrepreneurs. Some will even call them leaders. The common thread is always the same: they are solution seekers.

I am a doctor and an entrepreneur. Straddling the medical and business worlds can be challenging at times. I like to think this is why I am an Alpha. And to each challenge, I will find a solution.

I encourage each Alpha, entrepreneur, leader, doctor to think outside of the box and about what being an Alpha means to them. If you found a problem, then most likely others have experienced it too.

However, if you have an idea of how to solve that problem, it is unlikely someone else has thought of the exact same, or there would be some trail leading to it.

Follow your instincts, you might change the world for the better doing so. If not, you will have learnt much in the process. You will be changing the world for the better next time. And the next time is right around the corner when you are an Alpha!

> "Alphas feel the urge to talk at a population level because they gain satisfaction from impact."
> Dr. Jeremy Krell

Alpha, entrepreneurs, leaders, doctors, label them as you wish, they are the forces driving the world towards the future, they are solution seekers. My name is Dr. Jeremy Krell and I am an Alpha.

This is **AMONGST THE ALPHAS**.

Dr. BAK NGUYEN

CONCLUSION
BY DR. BAK NGUYEN

It feels so strange to me to conclude this book, almost 18 months after I've started the writing. After 2 weeks, I was done and ready to move on to the next book. Actually, I wrote volume one and two within a month, as my habits were propelling me.

Then, I waited for my co-authors to deliver. This has been the story of my life. I waited, waited and waited. And then, I moved on. What started as a rhetoric exercise of what is an Alpha got heavily tested as the world suddenly stops because of COVID.

As the world was standing still, some people reorganized, amongst them, there were **THE ALPHAS**. We were left standing, looking for ways to help one another and to see through the current situation and challenges. We made the most of what we could.

A year later, as I looked back on what we have achieved, I was stumped. We did so much, each in our own way and capability, but we all brought something to the *table of solutions*. In the midst of the actions, we needed a name, I threw in **THE ALPHAS** because that was the brand I was working on.

Well, 12 months later, THE ALPHAS is a strong brand, with values, members, and an international reputation. As I reopened my library of unpublished books, I rediscovered **AMONGST THE ALPHAS** volume one and two, left unfinished by my co-authors. I decided to edit the manuscripts and upgraded them to my new **ALPHA PROTOCOLS**.

I was speechless of how what I wrote a year ago has taken shape and materialized within the organization called THE ALPHAS. I never imposed my views on anyone, I simply host and unified those with a common desire and goal. And THE ALPHAS were born.

We are not the best nor the strongest nor the smartest. We are the first to respond. Not out of responsibility but out of nature, some will even say out of curiosity. That's our nature, to stand and seek as the needs arise.

As I said when we started this journey, not everyone is an Alpha but anyone can choose to embrace their *Alpha Gene*, that we all have within us. What is an Alpha, what is the responsibility and what do we eat in winter? Well, those are secondary, but also universal in definition. How can I be so sure?

Well, read my chapters and then, read the 6 Alphas who joined me on this journey. Between **AMONGST THE ALPHAS** volume one and two, we were strangers, coming from different cultures, generations, and continents, and yet, we all shared the same story, the same DNA.

I must add that even if only 7 of us joined the writing, you can interview any of the Alphas and you will have a unique story with the same spine, the same pattern. This gives me hope, much hope as I now have the confirmation that isolation can be broken.

And what did we do amongst Alphas? Did we tear each other apart to prove who was the strongest? No, we empowered one another, elevating both parties to a higher level of energy and to new horizons.

> "To empower is not to give power but to help discover the power that each has within."
> Dr. Bak Nguyen

Dr. Ouellette will be the first to concur with this affirmation. But so will Dr. Kunstadter, Dr. Krell, coach Jonas, and each of the Alphas. We came together and we build from the differences as well as from the common threads.

And what is it in this for you, any of you? Well, hope! The hope that it is possible to elevate yourself and to find support. We are not the only Alphas out there, many have preceded us, and even more will join.

> "To be an Alpha is a choice and a way of life. Life is Alpha, we were all born with the Alpha Gene."
> Dr. Bak Nguyen

If you were looking for hope, there it is. Because you are alive, you have the **Alpha Gene** in you. What you choose to do with it is another question. You've received life, so what now? Well, life and *Alphaness* are one and the same.

If you are still unsure and looking at your options, let me help you. We are social creatures. Amongst our basic needs, we need to gather and to interact with one another. The worldwide confinement and its restriction all reached us under our skin. That pain and depression we felt, were the craving for social interaction.

Only 2 things can happen as 2 or more people gather together. Either they connect and will raise the level of energy of each of the participants. Or, they can compare and lower the energy level of each of the parties.

Well, it is not entirely true. This is only an absolute when 2 people meet. As they connect, the energy is going up and as they compare, their energy will be going down. When 3 or more people are present, there is another possibility: 2 of them may connect as they are comparing themselves to the 3rd party. In that case, the 2 people connecting will feel a temporary increase of energy while the 3rd party will be left aside, falling into the *abyss*.

I just described here a classic high school scenario. Can this way of generating energy be sustainable? Well, what happened in high school? If gathering together and ridiculing someone else gave a temporary boost in energy and popularity, the only way to keep the energy up was to find a new target to repeat the same recipe.

Eventually, they run out of targets and will turn their nasty habit of **comparing** amongst themselves, **cannibalizing** one another. It is only a matter of time before this happens. The other side effect is even nastier.

As they are pointing fingers, they are also unifying all of those they are ridiculing. If they do not gain in numbers with a fast pace connecting with new people, eventually, they will be facing a crowd aligned against them, a crowd that they have created themselves. And this is often how bullies are taken down.

Well, Alphas are from a completely different species. 2 Alphas are not looking to take down the other since that won't help either party. They might get along, they might not, but fighting to prove a point isn't high on their list of priorities.

> "Alphas are solution seekers, not trouble makers."
> Dr. Bak Nguyen

I hope that I have helped establish the clear distinction of what is an Alpha and what folklore painted as a bully. On that, Dr. Kunstadter painted a different portrait: the Alpha is often the misfit and the one being pointed out as different.

Who are you? Look in the mirror and be honest with yourself. How many times did you hold back your opinions, fearing the judgment of others? Well, all these times, your *Alphaness* was crying for a chance to express itself.

Don't worry, even if you turned that voice down, which we all did somewhere in our life, that voice will raise again. The only difference is how well we have trained ourselves to listen or to ignore it. This is why I am stating that being an Alpha is a choice.

Being an Alpha is first and foremost to listen to your inner voice. if you listen to that voice, soon, you will feel the need to materialize your inner feelings and to walk your thoughts. It is there that you will appreciate the company of someone else following his or her inner voice, in other words, another Alpha.

Once in synergy, two Alphas can do much more in the presence of one another than the sum of what they could achieve by themselves. That's the **empowerment** factor in play. Empowerment and inspiration.

You see, that inner voice, that feeling was merely the beginning. As you have the chance to express it, and to have someone with whom will mirror your thoughts and energy, you will be reacting and will soon build on top of your original idea.

> "Hammering air three times over
> and it will become steel."
> Dr. Bak Nguyen

This is a quote from my first book, **SYMPHONY OF SKILLS**, written nearly 4 years ago. It makes even more sense today, in the presence of the ALPHAS. Take an idea, any idea, and express it amongst Alphas. Listen and exchange, and then, react to your own ideas. Do that 3 times over and you will be surprised how far and how fast you have moved forward.

This is why it is so important to stand amongst Alphas. If finding our voice alone was hard, the road ahead does not have to be as lonely. You just need to be open to connect.

Now, to attract an Alpha, you must be an Alpha too. And what is an Alpha? Someone open to share and to help, a solution seeker to used Dr. Krell's words.

This book started with Jonas' questions to explore what it is like to be different, to lead. Well, I am honored to report that Alphas are not different, just in a different state of mind.

> "Alpha is not a status nor a title but a choice. The rest is the line of consequences following one's choice."
> Dr. Bak Nguyen

If this is the end of this book, it is merely the beginning of a great and long journey. Mine and those of the Alphas joining to make the world a better place. Volume two is right around the corner with more Alpha guest authors joining. If volume one was more theoretical, volume two is all about personal experiences and growth.

And since I have edited these volumes months after I wrote them, I have a great surprise for all of you: after the series **AMONGST THE ALPHAS,** I have also completed a second series on the ALPHAS: **ALPHA LADDERS**.

Volume one co-written with coach Jonas Diop is already available. Volume two is waiting for my co-author Brenda Garcia to finish her chapters and it will reach the shelves soon.

This is 4 Alpha books within 18 months. With more and more Alphas joining, we have great hope for the future. History might say that COVID kickstarted **THE ALPHAS**.

To that, I will be grateful to History. What I must add is that COVID did not create THE ALPHAS, it just created the opportunity for ALPHAS to meet and exchange.

My name is Dr. Bak and I am an Alpha.

This is **AMONGST THE ALPHAS**.

May you find your power in the peace
of knowing what and who you really are

Dr. BAK NGUYEN

ABOUT THE AUTHORS

From Canada, **Dr BAK NGUYEN**, Nominee Ernst and Young Entrepreneur of the year, Grand Homage Lys DIVERSITY, and LinkedIn & TownHall Achiever of the year. Dr Bak is a cosmetic dentist, CEO and founder of Mdex & Co. His company is revolutionizing the dental field. Speaker and motivator, he wrote 72 books over 36 months accumulating many world records (to be officialized).

- **ENTREPRENEURSHIP**
- **LEADERSHIP**
- **QUEST OF IDENTITY**
- **DENTISTRY AND MEDICINE**
- **PARENTING**
- **CHILDREN BOOKS**
- **PHILOSOPHY**

In 2003, he founded Mdex, a dental company upon which in 2018, he launched the most ambitious private endeavour to reform the dental industry, Canada wide. Philosopher, he has close to his heart the quest of happiness of the people surrounding him, patients and colleagues alike. In 2020, he launched an International collaborative initiative named **THE ALPHAS** to share knowledge and for Entrepreneurs and Doctors to thrive through the Greatest Pandemic and Economic depression of our time.

In 2016, he co-found with Tranie Vo, Emotive World Incorporated, a tech research company to use technology to empower happiness and sharing. U.A.X. the ultimate audio experience is the landmark project on which the team is advancing, utilizing the technics of the movie industry and the advancement in ARTIFICIAL INTELLIGENCE to save the book industry and to upgrade the continuing education space.

These projects have allowed Dr Nguyen to attract interests from the international and diplomatic community and he is now the center of a global discussion in the wellbeing and the future of the health profession. It is in that matter that he shares his thoughts and encourages the health community to share their own stories.

> "It's not worth it go through it alone! Together, we stand, alone, we fall."

Motivational speaker and serial entrepreneur, philosopher and author, from his own words, Dr Nguyen describes himself as a dentist by circumstances, an entrepreneur by nature and a communicator by passion.

He also holds recognitions from the Canadian Parliament and the Canadian Senate

ABOUT THE GUEST AUTHORS

From USA, **Dr. Maria Kunstadter**, Doctor of Dental Surgery, co-founder THE TELEDENTIST, the biggest TELEDENTISTRY provider in USA. Experienced President with a demonstrated history of working in the hospital & health care industry. Skilled in Customer Service, Sales, Strategic Planning, Team Building, and Public Speaking. Strong business development professional with a Doctor of Dental Surgery focused in Advanced General Dentistry from UMKC School of Dentistry.

From USA: **Dr. Paul Ouellette**, DDS, MS, ABO, AFAAID, WORLD TOP 100 DENTISTS, Former Associate Professor Georgia School of Orthodontics and Jacksonville University. A visionary man looking for the future of our profession. Dr. Paul Ouellette Highly motivated to help my sons become successful in the "Ouellette Family of Dentists" Group Dental Specialty Practice.

From USA, **Dr. Jeremy Krell**, dentist MBA and serial entrepreneur, the real definition of an OVERACHIEVER. Highly experienced innovator and entrepreneur with a proven track record of taking early-stage startups to acquisition (multi-million dollar buyout). Excellent clinical dentistry and communication skills with in-depth analytical, organizational, and problem-solving abilities. A detail orientated and strategic leader in a dynamic, expeditious innovative environment. Firm experience with strategy, positioning companies, leading & developing teams, raising capital, investor relations, dental materials & techniques, negotiating & closing deals, and sales.

www.DrBakNguyen.com

AMAZON - BARNES & NOBLE - APPLE BOOKS - KINDLE
SPOTIFY - APPLE MUSIC

ULTIMATE AUDIO EXPERIENCE

A new way to learn and enjoy Audiobooks. Made to be entertaining while keeping the self-educational value of a book, UAX will appeal to both auditive and visual people. UAX is the blockbuster of the Audiobooks.

UAX will cover most of Dr Bak's books, and is now negotiating to bring more authors and more titles to the UAX concept. Now streaming on Spotify, Apple Music and available for download on all major music platforms. Give it a try today!

AMAZON - BARNES & NOBLE - APPLE BOOKS - KINDLE
SPOTIFY - APPLE MUSIC

COMBO
PAPERBACK/AUDIOBOOK
ACTIVATION

Please register your book to receive the link to your audiobook version. Register at: https://baknguyen.com/amongst-the-alphas-registry

Your license of the audiobook allows you to share with up to 3 peoples the audiobook contained at this link. Book published by Dr. Bak publishing company. Audiobook produced by Emotive World Inc. Copyright 2021, All right reserved.

FROM THE SAME AUTHOR
Dr Bak Nguyen

IT IS AVAILABLE AT

www.DrBakNguyen.com

MAJOR LEAGUES' ACCESS

FACTEUR HUMAIN -035
LE LEADERSHIP DU SUCCÈS
par Dr. BAK NGUYEN & CHRISTIAN TRUDEAU

ehappyPedia -038
THE RISE OF THE UNICORN
BY Dr. BAK NGUYEN & Dr. JEAN DE SERRES

CHAMPION MINDSET -039
LEARNING TO WIN
BY Dr. BAK NGUYEN & CHRISTOPHE MULUMBA

THE RISE OF THE UNICORN 2 -076
eHappyPedia
BY Dr BAK NGUYEN & Dr JEAN DE SERRES

BRANDING DrBAK -044
BALANCING STRATEGY AND EMOTIONS
BY Dr. BAK NGUYEN

002 - **La Symphonie des Sens**
ENTREPREUNARIAT
par Dr. BAK NGUYEN

006 - **Industries Disruptors**
BY Dr .BAK NGUYEN

007 - **Changing the World from a dental chair**
BY Dr. BAK NGUYEN

008 - **The Power Behind the Alpha**
BY TRANIE VO & Dr. BAK NGUYEN

036 - **SELFMADE**
GRATITUDE AND HUMILITY
BY Dr. BAK NGUYEN

072 - **THE U.A.X. STORY**
THE ULTIMATE AUDIO EXPERIENCE
BY Dr. BAK NGUYEN

088 - **CRYPTOCONOMICS 101**
MY PERSONAL JOURNEY
FROM 50K TO 1 MILLION
BY Dr BAK NGUYEN

BUSINESS

SYMPHONY OF SKILLS -001
BY Dr. BAK NGUYEN

CHILDREN'S BOOK
with William Bak

The Trilogy of Legends

THE LEGEND OF THE CHICKEN HEART -016
LA LÉGENDE DU COEUR DE POULET -017
BY Dr. BAK NGUYEN & WILLIAM BAK

THE LEGEND OF THE LION HEART -018
LA LÉGENDE DU COEUR DE LION -019
BY Dr. BAK NGUYEN & WILLIAM BAK

THE LEGEND OF THE DRAGON HEART -020
LA LÉGENDE DU COEUR DE DRAGON -021
BY Dr. BAK NGUYEN & WILLIAM BAK

WE ARE ALL DRAGONS -022
NOUS TOUS, DRAGONS -023
BY Dr. BAK NGUYEN & WILLIAM BAK

THE 9 SECRETS OF THE SMART CHICKEN -025
LES 9 SECRETS DU POULET INTELLIGENT -026
BY Dr. BAK NGUYEN & WILLIAM BAK

THE SECRET OF THE FAST CHICKEN -027
LE SECRETS DU POULET RAPIDE -028
BY Dr. BAK NGUYEN & WILLIAM BAK

THE LEGEND OF THE SUPER CHICKEN -029
LA LÉGENDE DU SUPER POULET -030
BY Dr. BAK NGUYEN & WILLIAM BAK

031- **THE STORY OF THE CHICKEN SHIT**
032- **L'HISTOIRE DU CACA DE POULET**
BY Dr. BAK NGUYEN & WILLIAM BAK

033- **WHY CHICKEN CAN'T DREAM?**
034- **POURQUOI LES POULETS NE RÊVENT PAS?**
BY Dr. BAK NGUYEN & WILLIAM BAK

057- **THE STORY OF THE CHICKEN NUGGET**
083- **HISTOIRE DE POULET: LA PÉPITE**
BY Dr. BAK NGUYEN & WILLIAM BAK

082- **CHICKEN FOREVER**
084- **POULET POUR TOUJOURS**
BY Dr BAK NGUYEN & WILLIAM BAK

THE SPIES AND ALIENS COLLECTION

077- **THE VACCINE**
079- **LE VACCIN**
077B- **LA VACUNA**
BY Dr BAK NGUYEN & WILLIAM BAK
TRANSLATION BY BRENDA GARCIA

DENTISTRY

PROFESSION HEALTH - TOME ONE -005
THE UNCONVENTIONAL
QUEST OF HAPPINESS
BY Dr. BAK NGUYEN, Dr. MIRJANA SINDOLIC,
Dr. ROBERT DURAND AND COLLABORATORS

HOW TO NOT FAIL AS A DENTIST -047
BY Dr. BAK NGUYEN

SUCCESS IS A CHOICE -060
BLUEPRINTS FOR HEALTH
PROFESSIONALS
BY Dr. BAK NGUYEN

RELEVANCY - TOME TWO -064
REINVENTING OURSELVES TO SURVIVE
BY Dr. BAK NGUYEN & Dr. PAUL OUELLETTE AND
COLLABORATORS

MIDAS TOUCH -065
POST-COVID DENTISTRY
BY Dr. BAK NGUYEN, Dr. JULIO REYNAFARJE AND
Dr. PAUL OUELLETTE

THE POWER OF DR -066
THE MODERN TITLE OF NOBILITY
BY Dr. BAK NGUYEN, Dr. PAVEL KRASTEV AND
COLLABORATORS

QUEST OF IDENTITY

004- **IDENTITY**
THE ANTHOLOGY OF QUESTS
BY Dr. BAK NGUYEN

011- **HYBRID**
THE MODERN QUEST OF IDENTITY
BY Dr. BAK NGUYEN

LIFESTYLE

045- **HORIZON, BUILDING UP THE VISION**
VOLUME ONE
BY Dr. BAK NGUYEN

048- **HORIZON, ON THE FOOTSTEPS OF TITANS**
VOLUME TWO
BY Dr. BAK NGUYEN

068- **HORIZON, DREAMING OF TRAVELING**
VOLUME THREE
BY Dr. BAK NGUYEN

MILLION DOLLAR MINDSET

MOMENTUM TRANSFER -009
BY Dr. BAK NGUYEN & Coach DINO MASSON

LEVERAGE -014
COMMUNICATION INTO SUCCESS
BY Dr. BAK NGUYEN AND COLLABORATORS

HOW TO WRITE A BOOK IN 30 DAYS -042
BY Dr. BAK NGUYEN

POWER -043
EMOTIONAL INTELLIGENCE
BY Dr. BAK NGUYEN

HOW TO WRITE A SUCCESSFUL BUSINESS PLAN -049
BY Dr BAK NGUYEN & ROUBA SAKR

MINDSET ARMORY -050
BY Dr. BAK NGUYEN

MASTERMIND, 7 WAYS INTO THE BIG LEAGUE -052
BY Dr. BAK NGUYEN & JONAS DIOP

PLAYBOOK INTRODUCTION -055
BY Dr. BAK NGUYEN

PLAYBOOK INTRODUCTION 2 -056
BY Dr. BAK NGUYEN

062- **RISING**
TO WIN MORE THAN YOU ARE AFRAID TO LOSE
BY Dr. BAK NGUYEN

067- **TORNADO**
FORCE OF CHANGE
BY Dr. BAK NGUYEN

071- **BOOTCAMP**
BOOKS TO REWRITE MINDSETS INTO WINNING STATES OF MIND
BY Dr. BAK NGUYEN

078- **POWERPLAY**
HOW TO BUILD THE PERFECT TEAM
BY Dr. BAK NGUYEN

PARENTING

024- **THE BOOK OF LEGENDS**
BY Dr. BAK NGUYEN & WILLIAM BAK

041- **THE BOOK OF LEGENDS 2**
BY Dr. BAK NGUYEN & WILLIAM BAK

086- **THE BOOK OF LEGENDS 3**
THE END OF THE INNOCENCE AGE
BY Dr. BAK NGUYEN & WILLIAM BAK

PERSONAL GROWTH

REBOOT -012
MIDLIFE CRISIS
BY Dr. BAK NGUYEN

HUMILITY FOR SUCCESS -051
BALANCING STRATEGY AND EMOTIONS
BY Dr. BAK NGUYEN

THE ENERGY FORMULA -053
BY Dr. BAK NGUYEN

AMONGST THE ALPHA -058
BY Dr. BAK NGUYEN & COACH JONAS DIOP

AMONGST THE ALPHA vol.2 -059
ON THE OTHER SIDE
BY Dr. BAK NGUYEN & COACH JONAS DIOP

THE 90 DAYS CHALLENGE -061
BY Dr. BAK NGUYEN

EMPOWERMENT -069
BY Dr BAK NGUYEN

THE MODERN WOMAN -070
TO HAVE IT HAVE WITH NO SACRIFICE
BY Dr. BAK NGUYEN & Dr. EMILY LETRAN

ALPHA LADDERS -075
CAPTAIN OF YOUR DESTINY
BY Dr BAK NGUYEN & JONAS DIOP

080- **1SELF**
REINVENT YOURSELF
FROM ANY CRISIS
BY Dr BAK NGUYEN

THE LAZY FRANCHISE

089- **THE CONFESSION OF
A LAZY OVERACHIEVER**
BY Dr BAK NGUYEN

090- **TO OVERACHIEVE
EVERYTHING BEING LAZY**
CHEAT YOUR WAY TO SUCCESS
BY Dr BAK NGUYEN

PHILOSOPHY

003- **LEADERSHIP** -003
PANDORA'S BOX
BY Dr. BAK NGUYEN

015- **FORCES OF NATURE**
FORGING THE CHARACTER
OF WINNERS
BY Dr BAK NGUYEN

040- **KRYPTO**
TO SAVE THE WORLD
BY Dr. BAK NGUYEN & ILYAS BAKOUCH

ALPHA LADDERS 2 -081
SHAPING LEADERS AND ACHIEVERS
BY Dr BAK NGUYEN & BRENDA GARCIA

MIRROR -085
BY Dr BAK NGUYEN

THE POWER OF YES

SOCIETY

010 - **THE POWER OF YES**
VOLUME ONE: IMPACT
BY Dr BAK NGUYEN

LE RÊVE CANADIEN -013
D'IMMIGRANT À MILLIONNAIRE
par DR BAK NGUYEN

037 - **THE POWER OF YES 2**
VOLUME TWO: SHAPELESS
BY Dr BAK NGUYEN

CHOC -054
LE JARDIN D'EDITH
par DR BAK NGUYEN

046 - **THE POWER OF YES 3**
VOLUME THREE: LIMITLESS
BY Dr BAK NGUYEN

AFTERMATH -063
BUSINESS AFTER THE GREAT PAUSE
BY Dr BAK NGUYEN & Dr ERIC LACOSTE

087 - **THE POWER OF YES 4**
VOLUME FOUR: PURPOSE
BY Dr BAK NGUYEN

TOUCHSTONE -073
LEVERAGING TODAY'S
PSYCHOLOGICAL SMOG
BY Dr BAK NGUYEN & Dr KEN SEROTA

091 - **THE POWER OF YES 5**
VOLUME FIVE: ALPHA
BY Dr BAK NGUYEN

COVIDCONOMICS -074
THE GENERATION AHEAD
BY Dr BAK NGUYEN

092 - **THE POWER OF YES 6**
VOLUME SIX: PERSPECTIVE
BY Dr BAK NGUYEN

TITLES AVAILABLE AT
www.DrBakNguyen.com

AMAZON - BARNES & NOBLE - APPLE BOOKS - KINDLE
SPOTIFY - APPLE MUSIC

www.ingramcontent.com/pod-product-compliance
Lightning Source LLC
Chambersburg PA
CBHW070338240426
43665CB00045B/2200